'The Mindful Manifesto helps us to "be" more and to "do" less. It's old wisdom backed by modern science, beautifully described.'

– Professor Richard Layard, Well-Being Programme Director,
London School of Economics

'This book is really important. Mindfulness is the way forward for dealing with depression and anxiety, and for general wellbeing.'

– Ruby Wax, comedian

'Every single person, from Prime Ministers and Presidents up to "ordinary men and women", would benefit from practising mindfulness and stillness in their lives. This wisdom has been known for thousands of years and now the science has at last caught up with it. This book makes the case admirably clearly.'

– Dr Anthony Seldon, Master of Wellington College and author of
Blair, Blair Unbound: The Biography Part II, Brown at 10 *and* Trust:
How We Lost It and How to Get It Back

'Wise, sensible and helpful for all forms of emotional disorders from depression to anxiety and addiction. This book on mindfulness is a great step towards finding peace of mind.'

– Sally Brampton, author of
Shoot the Damn Dog: A Memoir of Depression

'The Mindful Manifesto offers a fresh perspective on ancient wisdom. It is authentic, timely and hugely needed.'

– Peter J. Conradi, author of Going Buddhist: Panic and Emptiness,
the Buddha and Me *and* Iris Murdoch: A Life

'A lucid and highly practical guide to how the Buddhist techniques of mindfulness can be of enormous benefit to our health, relationships and peace of mind.'

– *Mick Brown, author of* The Spiritual Tourist: A Personal Odyssey Through the Outer Reaches of Belief *and* The Dance of 17 Lives: The Incredible True Story of Tibet's 17th Karmapa

'Is there anything worth doing that wouldn't go better if you practised mindfulness? Ed and Jonty have written a wonderful, accessible book that could save your health and change your life.'

– *Michael Chaskalson, co-author of* Mindfulness and Money, *honorary research fellow at the Centre for Mindfulness Research and Practice, Bangor University*

'A thoroughly well-written book that will serve as an excellent guide for anyone wishing to understand or practise mindfulness.'

– *Dr David Hamilton, author of* How Your Mind Can Heal Your Body *and* Why Kindness Is Good for You

THE MINDFUL MANIFESTO

THE MINDFUL MANIFESTO

HOW DOING LESS AND NOTICING MORE CAN HELP US THRIVE IN A STRESSED-OUT WORLD

DR JONTY HEAVERSEDGE & ED HALLIWELL

www.themindfulmanifesto.com

HAY HOUSE

Australia • Canada • Hong Kong • India
South Africa • United Kingdom • United States

First published and distributed in the United Kingdom by:
Hay House UK Ltd, 292B Kensal Rd, London W10 5BE. Tel.: (44) 20 8962 1230; Fax: (44) 20 8962 1239. www.hayhouse.co.uk

Published and distributed in the United States of America by:
Hay House, Inc., PO Box 5100, Carlsbad, CA 92018-5100. Tel.: (1) 760 431 7695 or (800) 654 5126; Fax: (1) 760 431 6948 or (800) 650 5115. www.hayhouse.com

Published and distributed in Australia by:
Hay House Australia Ltd, 18/36 Ralph St, Alexandria NSW 2015. Tel.: (61) 2 9669 4299; Fax: (61) 2 9669 4144. www.hayhouse.com.au

Published and distributed in the Republic of South Africa by:
Hay House SA (Pty), Ltd, PO Box 990, Witkoppen 2068. Tel./Fax: (27) 11 467 8904. www.hayhouse.co.za

Published and distributed in India by:
Hay House Publishers India, Muskaan Complex, Plot No.3, B-2, Vasant Kunj, New Delhi – 110 070. Tel.: (91) 11 4176 1620; Fax: (91) 11 4176 1630. www.hayhouse.co.in

Distributed in Canada by:
Raincoast, 9050 Shaughnessy St, Vancouver, BC V6P 6E5. Tel.: (1) 604 323 7100; Fax: (1) 604 323 2600

A catalogue record for this book is available from the British Library.

ISBN 978-1-84850-194-2

Printed in the UK by CPI William Clowes Ltd, Beccles, NR34 7TL.

This paper is manufactured from material sourced from forests certified according to strict environmental, social and economical standards.

CONTENTS

FOREWORD

There comes a time when any secret will get out into the world. No matter how hard we try to keep it hidden, it will be revealed, made manifest. For centuries, the principles and practices of mindfulness meditation were pretty much hidden away. You had to travel a far distance, perhaps to Asia, to see a teacher who might help you with the inner work of this meditation.

In the 1960s there was some excitement when certain forms of concentration meditation were taught in the West. Western scientists were intrigued: What were the psychological and physiological effects of such practices? The new scientific instruments of the day were used to measure bodily reactions such as heart rate and minor fluctuations in sweating. They showed that these meditations were as effective as deep relaxation techniques in calming the mind and body, and bringing about states of wellbeing.

But that's as far as it went. Because commonly used relaxation procedures were just as effective, anything 'extra' about the meditation was deemed to be unnecessary. Why recite mantras when identical effects could be found without them? Meditation as a 'technique' for reducing stress was reduced to a minority activity within science, and pursued by a relatively small group of distinguished Western scientists.

Then something changed. Because we are still living through the effects of this change, we can't be sure exactly what happened, but the dispersion of Tibetan and Vietnamese monks in the second half of the 20th century may lie at its root. The West had been prepared for this, in some ways, from the interest in Zen that had been an important cultural influence in the United States from the 1950s onwards. Also influential were some Western teachers who travelled to Asia (especially Thailand and Burma) and brought back to the West a different emphasis – what they called Insight (or Mindfulness) Meditation.

Mindfulness meditation doesn't just emphasise focusing and refocusing attention on a single point, but invites people to combine this training with a receptive, open awareness that might, if cultivated, offer a direct sense of what is arising, moment by moment, in the external and internal world. It also offers a way of responding to these events, and our reactions to them, with open-hearted compassion.

Gradually the message became clearer: we don't need to 'get rid' of our stress, tiredness and sadness, but to see its patterns clearly, and meet it with an open and friendly curiosity. This is different from our habitual reaction, which is to react to something we don't like by either pushing it away or brooding about it. Because we have never been taught any other way to meet our distress, we don't realise how much our habits of avoidance or brooding are making things worse, turning momentary tiredness into exhaustion, momentary fear into chronic worry, and momentary sadness into chronic unhappiness and depression. So it isn't our fault that we end up exhausted, anxious or depressed. We have been given only one tool to deal with things we don't like: get rid, work harder, be better, be perfect – and if we fail to make things different, we too easily conclude that we are a failure as a person. This is a recipe for a troubled world. As Jon Kabat-Zinn has said, we need, literally and metaphorically, to come to our senses.

What seems to be changing is that people are grasping this new way of understanding – the way of mindfulness. People are seeing more clearly the origin of much of our suffering, how our own reactions can compound our distress, and the path that can free us. People are returning to some of the original Buddhist texts and, more importantly, the practices that have been passed down over 25 centuries. These, taught in a secular context, have been found in recent scientific studies to liberate people from their stress, anxiety and unhappiness in ways that seem to go beyond the usual results of existing psychological treatments. These studies find that mindfulness not only reduces negative mood and prevents future episodes of clinical depression, but also enhances wellbeing and quality of life, even in the most tragic circumstances, by allowing people to let go of avoidance and brooding, and by cultivating self-compassion.

This is ancient wisdom in the East. But it is a new discovery for the West, and brings with it all the challenges that come when the West 'gets' a 'new thing'. Yet there is something we can say for sure: something that was hidden is now being revealed. We can now grasp it, we can hold it in our hands … and the word for this (from *manus* – hand, and *festus* – grasped) is the familiar word: 'manifesto'.

It is wonderful that Jonty Heaversedge and Ed Halliwell have written this book to give freely of their own experience, and to share the tremendous possibilities that come with training the mind and body to do less and to notice more. Their manifesto, like all manifestos, is both a statement of the potential that lies in all of us and a call to action to realise that potential. In the case of mindfulness, this call to action is to live life, moment by moment, as if it really mattered.

– Professor Mark Williams, University of Oxford
Author of *The Mindful Way through Depression*

PREFACE

Our intention in writing this book is to offer some insight into what is meant by 'mindfulness' – its roots in meditation and Buddhism, its relevance to modern-day life and the increasing scientific basis for its use in optimising health and wellbeing. We would also like to share with you the experiences of some people who have benefitted from practising mindfulness, and to encourage you to try it for yourself.

We have tried to strike a balance between East and West, Buddhism and psychology, secular and spiritual, theoretical and experiential to make it as interesting as possible to as wide an audience as possible. We hope you will find this approach engaging and challenging in equal measure, and that it will stimulate you to investigate the subject further.

This is not a 'Buddhist' book and is not meant to challenge any religious (or non-religious) beliefs you may have. However, given how connected the practices of meditation and mindfulness are with the Buddhist tradition, we felt it important to offer some context and to show how current ideas about mindfulness evolved out of it. By combining both Buddhist philosophy and current scientific research in the fields of psychology, immunology and neuroscience, we hope you find what we have written both authentic and current.

We are only at the beginning of discovering how mindfulness could help us to live happier, more productive, compassionate and meaningful lives. Not only could the development of greater mindfulness help to reduce physical and mental health problems, free us from unwanted behaviours and improve our functioning in our relationships and jobs, but it is also a basis for understanding how to develop our potential as human beings. *The Mindful Manifesto*, then, is not just for people experiencing 'illness'; it is for anyone who wants to be happier and healthier and to live in a wiser, more peaceful, genuine and compassionate world.

Ed Halliwell and Jonty Heaversedge
August 2010

CHAPTER ONE

A CALL TO BEING

Just 'be' for a moment – focus your attention on what is happening in your body, in your mind, in the world around you – be inquisitive about whatever your experience is, and allow yourself to slow down enough to notice.

We live in an overactive world. From the moment we wake up, many of us are already started on a frantic round of relentless striving that ends only when we crash, exhausted, into bed at night. Whether we're trying to make money, raise kids, help friends, build a career, save the world, get a bigger house, faster car, stronger body or more attractive partner, it seems we are forever on the go, constantly trying to propel ourselves into a better future. We are doing, doing, doing – and we get stressed. Around 7 million adults in the UK are so tense that, if they saw a doctor, they'd be diagnosed with an anxiety disorder.[1]

There is nothing actually wrong with doing – it has enabled humanity to achieve some amazing feats. People have created machines that connect us to someone on the other side of the planet. They have made beautiful art, inspiring music, great literature and magnificent architecture. They have accumulated vast storehouses of knowledge that we can use to predict the weather, fly across the sky and carry out heart transplants. In the last 100 years especially, the speed at which we have made scientific and technological progress is astonishing. And that progress has given us the capacity to *do* even more, even faster. We can click a mouse, flick a switch, press a button and accomplish tasks that would have taken previous generations many times longer – if they could have managed them at all. Because of all this accomplishment, many of us lead lives that seem healthier, safer and more comfortable than our ancestors could have dared hope for.

But there is a problem. Despite all these incredible advances, are we really happy? After all, isn't the point of all this doing to make our lives easier, more enjoyable? Every time someone invents a quicker computer or develops a new medical treatment, isn't he or she trying to reduce the amount of hassle or suffering that we have to cope with in our lives? Unfortunately, the evidence speaks for itself: even for those of us who live in the Western world, in countries which boast the highest levels of material comfort, suffering is everywhere. Our health services are overwhelmed by patients with chronic illness. We are scared of crime and terrorism. Our relationships break down. Our children don't 'perform' at school. We get into conflict with neighbours. We work too hard, or not at all, or in a job we don't like.

And then there are the huge global challenges we face –
threats of war, poverty and environmental devastation,
for which we have yet to invent a solution. Sometimes our
inventions make the suffering even greater. The tremendous
technologies of the 20th century have undoubtedly saved
and improved lives, but they have also been used to kill
millions of people, as well as potentially creating a climate
catastrophe that threatens our very survival as a species.

Even on a mundane level, surveys tells us that the devices
designed to help us get things done faster (and therefore
give us more time) actually end up making us feel more
stressed.[2] We use gadgets to try and multitask, as fast as we
can, urgently processing the huge volumes of information
thrown at us from every direction. Speedy technology can
make us rush even faster, bombarding us with so much
choice we can no longer give anyone, or anything, our
undivided attention. We walk around with our headphones
in, send text messages to one friend while chatting to
another, answer the phone when we're eating a meal and
reply to office emails from the beach. We are so often
distracted.

We want to relieve the stress in our lives and the suffering
in our world, because we want to be happy. We want to be
less anxious and in less pain, we want to feel safe in our
neighbourhoods, we want a good relationship, we want our
children to do well at school and we want to have a good
career. We want to flourish. And so perhaps we do even
more, hoping that will make us feel better. We might go
to a different doctor, move house, change partners, or get
a new job – perhaps one that pays more money so we can

buy more 'stuff' which we think will bring us satisfaction. We'll take pills and potions, bend, stretch, diet and detox … if we only make enough of an effort, surely we will find the solution to our pain? We grit our teeth. Or perhaps we get busy in the other direction – distracting ourselves from our problems by drinking, smoking, taking drugs or overeating.

Some of us decide we want to do something to help other people. We want to cure cancer, so we decide to become a doctor or health researcher. We want to beat crime, so we join the police. We want to stop global warming, famine and war, so we recycle our plastic bags, give money to charity or go on marches. As the saying goes: 'Don't just sit there, do something.'

A few people want to do something so much that they go into politics. They devise and carry out programmes designed to solve our problems from above – improving the lot of communities, countries or even the planet. These programmes come from the left, right and middle of the political spectrum – from communists to capitalists, anarchists to army generals, religious people to humanists. The plans may differ in content, but the underlying message is usually the same: if we want to make the world a happier place, we need to do something – *right now!*

But what if all this doing is actually part of the problem? What if, rather than needing to take more action, we need to take less? What if our compulsive habit of striving so hard to make things better is actually part of the reason we are so anxious? What if we don't need technology to speed up, but ourselves to slow down? Could it be that by doing less, not more, we might actually begin to relieve our chronic illness and stress? What might happen if we decided just to accept things as they are, to just 'be' for a while? By learning how to slow down and pay more attention to our world, might we then see more clearly how to make it a happier place?

LEARNING TO *BE*

Learning how to *be* – doing less and noticing more – is what the Mindful Manifesto is all about. It isn't the usual kind of manifesto – there is no great plan to solve all our problems instantly. Instead, it is an invitation to stop doing, at least for a time, and learn how to *be*, right now, in the present moment.

The word 'manifesto' derives from the Latin verb *manifestare*, which means 'to show plainly'. In English, to manifest means 'to become apparent'. Our suggestion is that by learning how to *be,* we might start to release a deep wisdom that can show us plainly how things really are, and what we need to do, without the need for agendas of any kind. Things can become apparent, our deepest values will become clearer and we will begin to know what to do. By using the word manifesto in this way, we are reclaiming its true meaning – not a plan of action, but a call to being.

By learning how to *be*, we take our foot off the gas pedal of activity, come out of overdrive and restore some mental and physical balance. Rather than desperately searching for a cure for our problems, we let go and begin to let a natural wellbeing, wakefulness and wisdom emerge. We stop seeking answers, and let them come to us. We give up the fight – *and* the stress that comes with it.

This could relieve some of the chronic illness that afflicts so many of us. Mental health problems like depression and anxiety make up around 30 per cent of the average family doctor's caseload,[3] and the World Health Organisation has predicted that, within 20 years, depression will have become the planet's most burdensome illness.[4] And then there are the masses of stress-related physical symptoms that doctors are unable to diagnose or treat effectively. These 'medically unexplained illnesses' – such as chronic back, stomach or chest pain, irritable bowel syndrome and fatigue – are a factor in up to a third of GP consultations.[5]

Neither doctors nor patients like feeling powerless, and so we often try to deal with illnesses like these with *more* doing – trying a new drug or treatment, arranging a visit to a specialist or having tests done. Unfortunately, because stress and overactivity frequently cause these conditions, all this doing can actually make things worse, and everyone – doctor and patient – just becomes more and more frustrated.

Even when doctors *can* diagnose our problems, there's no guarantee of a cure. There are good treatments for infections and a number of cancers these days, but most illnesses that trouble us are chronic – we just have to learn to live with them. Unfortunately, the common assumption that doctors can 'fix' us is false.

So, instead of struggling with illness, perhaps we could accept it as a natural part of life? We may still take drugs, have surgery or try some other form of therapy – but by learning how to *be* with our condition, rather than fighting it so hard, we could reduce our stress, giving treatments the best chance to work, and ourselves the best chance of recovery.

Learning how to 'be' could improve more than just our health. It could impact our wellbeing on every level, as individuals, couples, families, communities, nations and as a world. Whether it's a difficult relationship, an addiction or the threat of war, we can allow space for solutions to emerge. As the dust created by our stress begins to settle, we can open up, relax into our situation and see more clearly. Wisdom can start to dawn, and we can begin to act creatively, decisively and appropriately, more spontaneously in tune with our world.

It sounds simple, doesn't it? And in a sense, it is – if we can truly relax, we will start to see things as they are, be fully ourselves, act more skilfully and find greater contentment. It doesn't even cost any money. Unfortunately, although it *is* simple, manifesting in this way is not easy. Try it for yourself and you might see what we mean. For the next two minutes, put this book down and don't do *anything*. Wherever you are, just 'be'.

THE HABIT OF BUSY-NESS

So, how was it? Maybe you were confused ('I'm not sure what I'm supposed to be doing – should something be happening here?'), irritated ('What a pointless exercise! Of course I know how to be – I'm being all the time, aren't I?') or excited ('Ah great, we're getting to the part where they tell me how I get better!')? Perhaps you got interrupted by someone who thought you were acting strangely, or who desperately wanted you to talk to them. Maybe you were distracted by the noise of a car, a beautiful flower, remembering you'd left the gas on, or a stomach ache. Or maybe you didn't do the exercise at all – you couldn't wait to get onto the next paragraph, or you just couldn't be bothered.

Whatever happened, we bet you didn't instantly find yourself feeling naturally wise, open and relaxed, or spontaneously in tune with your world. Why *is* 'being' so difficult? Surely it shouldn't be so hard to stop doing, just for two minutes?

It is difficult because we are not used to it. From the day we were born, we have been bombarded with stimuli that tell us we should keep busy. We have learned it from our parents, who were probably busy trying to keep it all together while we were growing up, and from our schools, which probably taught us that the way to survive in a busy world is to get busy ourselves. And we learn it from the media, which provides a constant stream of information, entertainment and drama, telling us all about how other people are busy – especially influential ones like politicians, sportspeople and celebrities. If we are busy, the message goes, we can become rich, and if we are rich we can afford things that will make us happy.

Most of us know that all this busy-ness is *not* the way to be happy. When someone actually stops and asks us what makes us feel content, we are prompted to reflect and we respond wisely. According to a Mental Health Foundation survey, 81 per cent of us agree that 'the fast pace of life and the number of things we have to do and worry about these days is a major cause of stress, unhappiness and illness in our society,' while 86 per cent agree that 'people would be much happier and healthier if they knew how to slow down and live in the moment.'[6] But still we don't do it – our busy-ness has become a habit. Meanwhile, the cult of doing is everywhere, making its lure difficult to resist. So we just carry on being speedy, even though somewhere deep down we know there is something wrong.

We are not only busy bodies, we are busy minds. In the same Mental Health Foundation survey, more than half the people said they 'find it difficult to relax or switch off, and can't stop thinking about things I have to do or nagging worries'. The messages telling us to keep busy are so powerful that they get ingrained in our thought patterns and drive our behaviour, even when it makes us mentally or physically ill. Even when we say we are 'doing nothing', what we often mean is that we are tuning out in front of the TV.

No wonder that one of the frequently heard cries from early 21st-century citizens is for some 'headspace'. We get stressed because there is often so little space in our minds. Unfortunately, because there is so little space, and because we are stressed, there is no room to reflect on how to find a way out of our predicament. The faster we go, the more we tend to react impulsively, following our unconscious, habitual patterns. It is a nasty vicious circle. And in order to release ourselves from it, we need help. We need a powerful antidote to speed. We need a method.

THE METHOD OF MINDFULNESS

One powerful method is mindfulness. In mindfulness meditation, we practise paying attention and notice what is happening in our body, our mind and the world around us. We slow down, deliberately and gently bringing awareness to our experience, over and over again. Gradually, as we practise, we begin to see how we get caught up with being on automatic pilot, unconsciously playing out habitual patterns of thought, feelings and behaviour that create stress and suffering. In mindfulness meditation, we start being fully present to our thoughts and feelings, and we create space in our mind and body.

By calmly, quietly and kindly observing our mind, we see our repetitive, negative thinking patterns, our uncomfortable feelings – anger, perhaps, sadness or fear – and we notice how they impel us towards reactions which cause us suffering, even though we hope they will make us happier.

In mindfulness meditation, we let go of action and watch our mind, with curiosity and friendliness. We notice how everything in it arises and passes away naturally – and we see that we don't have to be so caught up in everything we think, feel and do – we simply watch it all in a friendly, compassionate and interested way. We begin to see that we are not our thoughts and feelings, and that they do not have to dominate us – we stop taking things so personally. This is the foundation for a wiser, gentler, more compassionate and confident relationship with our minds, and with our lives.

Compare this mindful mode to our usual, overactive way of operating. When we are rushing through life, most of us aren't paying much attention at all. Instead, we're swept away by thoughts and feelings, shunted into reactions that are based on habit, the powerful impulse to continue doing what we did in the past.

When we have a negative thought, rather than watching it arise and dissolve, we dwell on it, create a story around it, and throw ourselves into a round of punishing criticism: 'I always feel so useless compared to Sally, she's so on top of things ... mind you, she's boring, she's got no life outside work ... oh great, there I go again, why am I so negative?' Or, when someone shouts at us, rather than observing the anger or fear it produces in our bodies, we shout back or run away. We rush around constantly, brooding about the past and worrying about the future. We keep on doing the same old things, and getting the same old results. This is mind*less*ness.

In mindfulness meditation we learn to tolerate our impulse to follow old patterns which don't serve us. We cultivate a gap between thought and action, in which we can simply be present to our experience. Gradually, as we become more and more skilled, our ability to dwell in this gap grows, and we are impelled less and less into impulsive, knee-jerk reactions. We can stay with our experience long enough to consider our options, connect with our deepest values and start to make wiser choices. We step out of automatic pilot. As we begin to make better decisions, our lives start to work better – we begin to exist in the flow of life, rather than always trying to resist it or escape it. By practising mindfulness, we are laying the ground for deep, lasting change, creating space in which we can develop new habits of thinking and behaving that will serve us better, and help us serve others better.

Mindfulness meditation is no quick fix – it means giving up the search for instant answers that come from outside us. It means taking a profound, radical step, starting to cut out suffering at its root – in our minds. This is supremely empowering – for while we may not appear to have full control over our external lives, we can always work with our mind, turning our attention to gently, firmly and repeatedly training it to thrive in the midst of life's challenges. We aren't just tinkering with what work we do, where we live, how much money we make or whom we decide to be friends with – we are changing how we relate with our consciousness, the tool that actually experiences all these details. By changing how we relate with our minds, we start to put wellbeing in our own hands.

It's a bit like having a TV with a fuzzy picture – it blurs, cuts out, and there's snow on the screen. You try changing channels, fiddling with the remote, switching it on and off again, or banging the set. Finally you call the engineer, who goes up on the roof and gently shifts the aerial – it had been forced out of place by the wind. Your reception becomes clearer.

Many of us deal with our problems in the same way: we try to change channels, hit the remote or bang the set – to alter the contents of our experience. With mindfulness meditation, we're learning how to change the position of our aerial, to see things from a different perspective. We're training our mind to receive the experience of our lives clearly and accurately.

PRACTISING GENTLY

If we practise mindfulness regularly, in a spirit of curiosity and gentleness, and without striving for results, the benefits will appear. We can start to see how our craving for pleasure causes us pain, and how our attempts to resist or escape suffering only make it greater. We may no longer be so in thrall to the conditioning we received when we were growing up, or so easily give in to the social and cultural pressures to speed up and follow the herd, doing things that aren't good for us, for others or for the world. Perhaps we'll start to see that we can't solve the problems of a busy mind with a busy mind.

Maybe we won't be so upset when things don't go right, and start to accept and be realistic about the natural ups and downs of human existence – life can become less of an insult and more of a joy. Mindfulness allows us to enjoy the delights of the world, without getting so attached to them or using them in a way that depletes the earth's resources. It can mean we unconsciously harm others less often. With mindfulness we can make better decisions, and no longer be so tempted to chase dreams that won't bring us happiness. We can start to choose consciously and cultivate behaviours that bring about genuine contentment. When we are mindful we spend less time living in our heads, and aren't so dominated by our thoughts and feelings – we become less wrapped up in ourselves. We can start to see and flow with the way things are. We can start to be!

Now, imagine if you weren't the only one who's decided to learn how to be more mindful. Imagine if all your friends and family decided to start practising meditation as well. Then it wouldn't only be you who noticed how habitual tendencies get in the way of wellbeing, and how constant craving and doing create more suffering. Everyone around you would slow down, start paying attention to their minds and begin to reap the benefits of greater awareness. They too might start to become more relaxed, and more discerning. Their discoveries about their minds could chime with your own insights, and you could start to feel supported by your environment rather than challenged by it. Your friends and family might feel the same, bringing you closer and allowing your lives to work in flow together. The energy of mindfulness would grow in power and, with increased confidence, you might feel more able, as a group, to resist the cultural and social pressures to be speedy and materialistic. You would all feel less stressed. You might each get ill less often, and start to feel happy more of the time, more able to share the joys of the world with one another. You would start living mindfully. You would start being, together.

And now, imagine that the news about the benefits of mindfulness meditation spread much, much further and wider. Imagine if instruction in mindfulness were available to every patient, with any health condition. Imagine that instead of telling us about the latest celebrity gossip, the latest car or the latest diet, newspapers and magazines used some space to inform their readers that developing and maintaining mindfulness practice could lead us towards a happier, healthier life. Imagine that instead of pressuring us to work harder and faster, employers encouraged their workers to take time out each day to meditate, in the knowledge that real productivity comes from a relaxed, clear-minded and energetic staff. Imagine if mindfulness were taught in every primary and secondary school, so that instead of just learning how to pass exams and reach targets, children discovered from an early age how to 'be', embedding their learning in a framework of greater compassion and creativity. And imagine, just imagine, if instead of shouting about how useless their opponents are, politicians sat mindfully in meditation for 10 minutes before each session of Parliament, pausing to disengage their egos and notice how their unhelpful old patterns of thought and feelings might be driving their decisions – shifting our current process of government away from defensiveness and confrontation and further towards constructive collaboration and cooperation. Imagine, finally, what it would be like if mindfulness formed the groundwork of our whole lives, the basis from which we could work towards creating the happy world that we all want, but which we seem to find so hard to manifest.

Unrealistic, you might say. Pie in the sky. A pipe dream. People would never do it – they already think they don't have enough time, so why would they sit down to practise meditation? Anyway, most people think meditating is a weird, 'new-age' thing, something to do with Eastern religion or escaping from reality. What's going to make them change their minds? I might give it a go – after all, that's why I picked up this book – but the idea that the majority of ordinary people are going to do it is a flight of fancy; it just isn't going to happen. And as for doctors, teachers, employers and politicians encouraging people to meditate – give me a break!

MINDFULNESS IN THE MAINSTREAM

If that's what you think, we have news for you. It's already starting to happen. Mindfulness meditation is no longer found only on the spiritual fringes, in self-help sections of bookshops and alternative health centres. It is going mainstream. Powerful people are starting to sit up and take notice, realising that mindfulness might be, as suggested, a way to work more skilfully with some of the enormous problems we face as a world.

Why are they taking notice now, you might ask, when meditation practitioners have long been saying that working with our minds in this way is beneficial? After all, mindfulness is not a new technology – the basic practices have been around for thousands of years.

The answer is *science*. Over recent years, a large and ever-growing volume of research has been backing up some of the claims that have been made about the benefits of mindfulness.[7] Pioneering psychologists have developed new therapies based around mindfulness practices, and carefully examined their effects to see if and how they work. Study after study has been published in reputable academic journals showing that practising mindfulness can indeed reduce stress, anxiety and depression, as well as strengthening the immune system, speeding healing and helping people to manage a wide range of physical illnesses.

Research has confirmed that mindfulness can sharpen our attention, concentration and memory, improve our emotional balance, help us to sleep better, boost our self-esteem, make us less angry and unleash our creativity. It has shown that mindfulness can reduce negative thinking and help us to enjoy more satisfying relationships with others. Neuroscientists have also shown that practising mindfulness can lead to positive changes in the brain, increasing activity and even promoting growth in areas of our neural networks associated with wellbeing.

Studies have also found that people who are more naturally mindful are less neurotic, less defensive and more extrovert, as well as having more energy and awareness, and being generally happier with their lives. When they do experience bad moods, they recover from them more quickly. They are more compassionate and empathic – mindful people care about others, and feel closer to and more connected with them.

We live in a scientific age, and when this kind of research demonstrates that something works, people in power take notice. That is understandable – the scientific method has led to many of the great achievements of the 'doing' world over the past few centuries, especially in areas such as medicine and health. When a few spiritual devotees or new-age dropouts were the only ones saying meditation is helpful, they were never going to convince the mainstream. But when reputable academics from universities like

Harvard and Oxford start saying the same thing, and providing the data to prove it, that's something entirely different. Some of their data has even shown that teaching people mindfulness could save us money – that kind of information really makes people in power prick up their ears!

Mindfulness is simple, and yet it can be used to help with so many different problems. The basic instruction on how to practise it can be given in just a few minutes, and can be learned by almost anyone. It can be done on the bus, in the supermarket, at your desk, in bed. You don't need any special equipment – just your mind! There probably isn't any situation in which more mindfulness wouldn't be helpful, from the smallest daily niggles to the largest global problems.

The idea that mindfulness could be the foundation for a happier life and a happier world isn't new, but because of all this scientific endeavour, it is now starting to reach some of the people who need it most. In the United States, mindfulness is already being taught in hundreds of hospitals, to people with conditions ranging from anxiety, fatigue and back pain to heart disease, HIV and cancer. Meanwhile in the UK, the Government has recently recommended mindfulness as a treatment for people who have repeated episodes of depression. GPs are becoming much more convinced about its benefits – the Mental Health Foundation survey mentioned earlier found that 68 per cent of British family doctors think it would be helpful for their patients to learn how to practise mindfulness. Programmes are also being developed to teach it to people with addictions, to pregnant women and their partners, to schoolchildren, and to couples who want to enjoy more harmonious relationships.

The seeds of a more mindful society are being planted, but there is still a way to go. While mindfulness is now quite well known and respected among health professionals, the chances of someone being referred for meditation training on the NHS are small. When we consider the number of people suffering from stress, depression and chronic physical ill-health, the services available are little more than a drop in the ocean.

The same is true in schools, workplaces, prisons and in government – there are exciting pilot schemes, but most people probably haven't heard about mindfulness, let alone tried to practise it.

WHAT IS MINDFULNESS?

Mindfulness is bringing attention to your present experience, on a moment-to-moment basis, in an inquisitive, non-critical way.

Most of us will have some idea of what it is to be mindful – of someone else's feelings, pedestrians crossing a busy road, or the step as you get off the train. We generally use 'mindful' to mean that we should pay particular attention to something or someone, to take care, or to notice what is going on around us. What may come as more of a surprise is that being mindful is a quality we can develop and train ourselves in, a tool we can use to cultivate greater balance and happiness.

In this book we are going to explore what is meant by mindfulness from both a Buddhist and a more scientific perspective. We will look at how it can be used to help train the mind, to change destructive ways of thinking and behaving, improve our physical and mental health, and allow us to thrive in our daily lives.

'Mindfulness' is one of those words that, the more you start to think about it, to unpick it, the more difficult it can be to define. It is a word that has many facets to it. Over recent times it has come to be used predominantly to describe a psychological approach to treating a range of health problems, and it is now understood by many merely as a therapeutic method. However, it would be a mistake to think of mindfulness simply as a psychological concept, or a process that is only beneficial in the treatment of stress or depression. It is much, much more than this. It is a way of experiencing ourselves, and the world we live in – a way of being – and one that has been recognised for thousands of years to promote physical, psychological and spiritual health. Mindfulness is an approach to life – it's about how we relate to ourselves and the world around us.

At one level, it is simply about staying with the present moment, paying attention to our mind, our body and our surroundings, in an inquisitive, non-judgemental way, and not getting distracted by our thoughts and feelings – our constant mental chatter – so that we can truly experience every situation for what it is, in a genuine, open and curious way. Over time we start to notice what's happening in our mind, to become familiar with it and the effect it has on us. Gradually, we then begin to recognise our thoughts for what they are – just thoughts. They are not 'us', they do not define us, they are not 'real' and they are not 'true' (or 'false', for that matter) – they are simply thoughts. This doesn't mean that they are not of value, but by not identifying with them or embroidering them with layer upon layer of emotion or meaning it is easier to let them go and pay attention to what's happening right now. Gradually, we can free ourselves from the limitations created by our habitual patterns of thinking and reacting to situations. Our thoughts lose their power to send us tumbling into despair, distract us with daydreams or blind us with longing, and we are able to make different choices about what we'd like to do.

We spend most of our lives on autopilot. Much of the time, we don't even notice what we are thinking, saying or doing – whether we are driving the car, listening to friends, taking a shower, eating our breakfast or making love. Practices involving mindfulness allow us to wake up to our experience, reconnect with a clearer, more spacious mind, and take a fresh approach to whatever comes up rather than falling back on our usual, habitual, mind*less* responses to situations.

So, mindfulness is not simply about 'not doing'; it's an active, purposeful process – there is effort involved. We have to constantly remember to pay attention. In fact, some definitions of mindfulness use the word 'remembering' – not what happened yesterday or last week, but rather on a moment-to-moment basis, 're-minding' ourselves to pay attention to where we are, what we are doing and whom we are with. This is what cognitive psychologists call our 'working memory' – our moment-to-moment memory lasting just a few seconds, which allows us to hold our attention on what we are doing. So when our mind wanders off and we forget where we are, what we are doing and why we are doing it – mindfulness 'brings us back'. As we get distracted by the future or the past, mindfulness helps us stay with the here and now. Meditation, and the other practices we are going to describe in this book, are ways of nurturing this quality.

We would sound a note of caution, however. This is not about never reflecting on the past or making plans for the future. It is also *not* about living 'for' the moment in a hedonistic sort of way. It is about living 'in' the moment, which will still involve making decisions and choices. This practice should not disempower us, or make us completely aimless. As we will see, it should allow us to make better, healthier, more intelligent choices for ourselves and our world. So it is not that in seeing thoughts as thoughts we treat their *content* non-judgementally – if we notice we are being hateful or causing harm, towards ourselves or others, there is little value in noticing it if we are not then able to bring our intelligence to bear and aim to do things differently in the future. The difference is that, simply by recognising our thoughts as thoughts and not over-identifying with them, we open up the possibility for just that – change.

If we are to have a hope of stemming the tide of chronic ill-health and unhappiness in our society; if we really want to live in a world that brings people happiness; if we really want to have a chance of tackling the mindlessness that causes so much stress and suffering, then more and more people will need to hear about the benefits of mindfulness. We will need to learn how to be mindful together.

That is why we have decided to write this book. We want to invite you to learn about mindfulness, and begin practising it for yourself. We want to invite you to step off the treadmill of manic doing and to investigate being. We don't promise instant results – indeed, if the practice is to work, you have to let go of goal-oriented craving and the need for quick solutions. But if you can do that, you can start to relax and enjoy the journey.

Practising mindfulness isn't always a comfortable experience. We have been rehearsing our habitual patterns for a long time, and they won't disappear overnight. We will still get caught up in our hopes, our fears and our speed, and we will still be impelled towards old habits. It may even be painful to see and experience these habits so clearly. But if you are motivated, the fresh perspective you develop can begin to bear fruit – your mind will start to loosen up and your habits will weaken their grip on your life. You will be able to be present more often, and to be more confident, open and relaxed.

Then you can take your practice out into your life, and start being more mindful in your family, community and workplace. Others may see how you are growing, and be intrigued by what you have been doing. And, when you tell them, some of them may be inspired to start practising themselves.

Gradually, as people join in, mindfulness could start to reach more people in every sphere of life – including employers, newspaper editors, teachers, healthcare commissioners and politicians. As more people manifest mindfulness in their lives, our collective stress levels could begin to fall, our communities could grow stronger and our world could become a more peaceful place.

The Mindful Manifesto, then, is not just a self-help book. Helping ourselves isn't quite enough – unless, of course, we plan to go off and meditate by ourselves in a cave forever, shielding ourselves from outside pressures. For most of us, that is neither possible nor desirable – we want to live with other people, and we want to try and make the world a better place.

By working with others to help create a more mindful environment, we make it easier to be mindful ourselves. If the world continues to push us in the direction of mind*less*ness, it will be much harder to keep from falling into old habits. But if we can be more mindful in our own lives, and by our example encourage others to do the same, we will start to create a virtuous circle to counter the vicious circle of speed.

MAKING A DIFFERENCE

Things won't change radically overnight, but if we are patient, we *can* begin to make a difference. We can be part of a shift in balance from doing to being, a new 'non-movement' of people willing to stop, even just for a short period each day.

But let's not go too fast. We don't need to try to improve things through force of will, or through more overactivity – that is not how mindfulness works. Change can come, but not through the exposition of grand theories, or carrying out great programmes of action. In time, we will know what action to take. First of all, don't just do something, sit there!

What can you expect from *The Mindful Manifesto*? We would like to share with you where mindfulness has come from – its roots in spiritual practices dating back thousands of years. We will look at how mindfulness is a lynchpin of ancient Buddhist teachings on how to relieve suffering. We will then explain how it came to the West in the late 20th century and was adapted to help patients suffering from chronic illness. We will show you how mindfulness affects the body, and how practising it can reduce your stress levels and help you cope with physical health problems.

Then we will tell the story of how psychologists working in mental health discovered mindfulness in the mid-1990s, and about the remarkable success of this 'new' treatment that has helped people who are prone to depression. We will also look at neuroscientific research that suggests that mindfulness actually alters, for the good, the way our brain works.

Next we will show how mindfulness can be used to help treat addictions, and how you can develop a greater ability to let go of destructive behaviours. And we will see how mindfulness can help you to be more effective and happy in other aspects of your life, such as at work, or in your relationships.

Finally, we will look at the big picture – how mindfulness can be a tool for manifesting our greater potential as human beings, how it can facilitate a saner approach to social problems and help us meet the myriad challenges of the 21st century.

All the way through we will be sharing our own experiences, the stories of people whose lives have been helped by mindfulness, and giving you tips and suggestions on how you can begin to develop your own practice.

We won't pretend that following the path of mindfulness is easy. It requires patience, discipline, energy and compassion. Sometimes it may seem frustrating, boring or confusing – and sometimes it may seem like nothing much is happening at all. But gradually, gently and unmistakably, if we practise together, we can become less busy and stressed, and create a healthier, saner world.

Before we go any further, we thought it might be helpful to share how we have become confident about the benefits of mindfulness. First, there is our professional experience. As a GP, Jonty sees people in his surgery every day, suffering from illnesses that are either caused or made worse by stress. And through his research and writing, Ed has studied and become more and more conscious of how the pressure to be overactive is at the root of so many of our problems. Through our jobs, we have each come to see again and again how relentless pressure creates enormous pain and suffering in people's lives. We have studied the scientific research, and we have seen people who are enormously helped by learning how to practise mindfulness – their anxiety levels fall, their conditions become more manageable and they can thrive, despite often very serious health problems.

Above all, we have become convinced because we have both benefited from mindfulness ourselves.

We both experience the pressure to do, achieve and consume that is endemic in our society, and we are both vulnerable to that pressure, and the stress it creates. We both find that meditation is an immensely powerful antidote. It's not a miracle cure, but a way of working with our experience that is both simple and effective. Below is a short summary of how each of us came to this conclusion, and how it continues to work in and on our lives.

Jonty's Experience

I first came across mindfulness and meditation about eight years ago. I had just turned 30 and there was a lot to celebrate. I was progressing well in a fulfilling career as a GP, I had good friends and no particular financial concerns. I should have felt a sense of achievement, but instead, in my mind I felt stuck. I was unhappy and didn't know why.

I didn't feel like I was depressed and I knew I didn't need to take any medication, but I also realised that I needed help to untangle the knot in my mind. I started seeing a psychotherapist who was incredibly helpful but, as therapy came to an end, I felt I wanted to find some way of working with my mind by myself. So I began to investigate meditation.

Like most people, when I first heard about meditation I made a whole range of assumptions – and my friends all joked about the idea of me sitting cross-legged and eating lentils (neither of which are necessary to practise being mindful!). For me the biggest resistance I had was to its origins in Buddhism. I had no real understanding of Buddhist beliefs, but I was worried about getting involved in anything 'religious'. As a GP I try to take a scientific approach to life and, whilst I respect people from all faiths and traditions, I wanted something that I could question and that could offer me some *evidence* of its benefits – both personally and professionally.

I was lucky enough to find the Shambhala Meditation Centre in London. It offered a more secular approach to meditation, and the teachers there were completely open to my process of exploration.

Whilst psychotherapy was the first step in changing my relationship with myself, meditation has offered me a very practical technique for continued observation and reflection in my life and, whilst I would still not say that I am 'a Buddhist', the knowledge and wisdom I have encountered throughout this process has provided a structure that has not only helped me to calm my mind, but also understand more about its nature … something that offers me great reassurance as I continue to notice more and more of my own neurotic tendencies!

I haven't become a new person. I am, however, more able to notice how I think and what I do, and the impact this has on me and the people around me. And the biggest difference is that I do this with more compassion and humour and less judgement and self-criticism than I used to. I am able to be inquisitive about my life without feeling driven to try and solve every problem I encounter, and without feeding the constant cycle of self-improvement that I so easily get trapped in.

Initially I found meditation uncomfortable, both mentally and physically. Just sitting still, noticing and letting go was so different to my usual energetic, solution-focused approach to life. I found the practice incredibly frustrating (and still do a lot of the time!). However, as time passed I began to notice differences in the way I handled situations at work, in my confidence in relationships and, most wonderfully of all, in my ability to connect with my patients. I was able to be more attentive and more available to them in consultations as I became less distracted by all the other thoughts jockeying for my attention. As I started to meditate regularly I found myself more able to be present in every situation that I encountered, both in and out of work. This is not always comfortable – mindfulness allows us to start seeing things as they are rather than as we would like them to be – but it enables us to bring our intelligence and our heart to bear in whatever situation comes our way. This offers me the opportunity to remove my metaphorical blinkers, and to be creative, equitable and compassionate in my responses, rather than simply reacting with my usual habitual defensiveness to new challenges.

I have seen how helpful these practices have been in my life – in my relationship with myself and other people, in my ability to take care of myself, my patients, my family and my friends, in the courage it has given me to say 'yes' to things I would previously have been too frightened to agree to (whether it has involved appearing on TV in front of millions of people or even writing a book!), and to say 'no' to things I would usually feel too insecure to refuse.

Ed's Experience

Learning how to practise meditation was the turning point that led me to recovery from a period of chronic depression and anxiety that had lasted nearly three years. After working speedily, busily and mindlessly in a media career that brought plenty of material benefits, I had suddenly collapsed under the weight of stress. Signed off work, I was miserable and frightened.

I thought the way to deal with my problems was to *do* something. And at that point I was so anxious I was willing to try anything. Within a few months, I had enough psychology and self-help books to start a small library. I was seeing a therapist, taking anti-depressants, attending support groups and seminars, and having all sorts of alternative treatments. I tried changing friends, changing jobs, changing where I lived – but none of it seemed to make much difference. In fact, it just made me feel more powerless.

By seeking answers with the desperate speed that had led to my crisis, I was perpetuating the same old patterns – if only I could just keep trying harder, I thought, I would be able to shake myself out of misery. In amongst all my books were some about meditation. People suggested it might be helpful for me, so I went to a local centre that offered instruction.

Initially, I approached the practice in the same way as all my other 'fixes' – throwing myself at it in the hope that I had finally found the answer. But there is something very clever about meditation – it's impossible to follow the instructions properly and chase after results at the same time. Soon, the penny started to drop – it was not so much *what* I was doing that was the problem, as *how* my mind worked – it was going way too hard, way too fast. In meditation, I saw my habitual patterns of speed and impulsive doing for the first time. I let go – at least a little bit. After a few months of meditating every day, my depression and anxiety began to lift.

I'm still prone to getting 'speedy' and so I've continued to practise – habitual patterns are hard to let go of. But gradually, the bouts of mental ill-health that used to be so regular and debilitating have begun to diminish, both in frequency and duration.

CHAPTER TWO

TAKING A DEEP BREATH

To become more fully aware of the remarkable experience of being alive, take some time every day to be mindful of your breath ...

Are you aware of your breathing, right now, as you read these words? We mean, are you *really* aware of the direct *experience* of your breathing, as it happens, in your body, and not just as the thought, 'Yes, of course I'm breathing'? Are you aware of the air brushing lightly against the inside of your nostrils as you take an in-breath? Do you feel the movement of your chest as it begins to expand? Can you feel the beat of your heart as it pumps oxygenated blood through your body? Now, do you feel your breath again as you exhale, the fall of your chest as it contracts, the light breeze on your face as the air mixes once more with the space around you?

See if you can pay attention to your breathing with this kind of attention, just for a minute or two. Place your mind gently on your breath, and follow its movement, in and out, as you adopt an attitude of friendly curiosity. See if you can really *be with* your breathing, and *know* that you are alive, not just as an intellectual idea, but with all your being. Notice how the breath feels in your body: does it produce any particular sensations? If so, whereabouts do you feel them? There's no need to analyse – just noticing is fine.

Amazing, really, isn't it? Throughout the day and night, our body keeps on breathing like this, whether we are aware of it or not. Even when we fall asleep or are unconscious, we are drawing air in, filling our lungs, feeding our organs – our bodies keep us alive. We don't need to do anything to make this happen, we can just *allow* it to happen. Our bodies breathe for us. It's pretty miraculous.

How often do you really *pay attention* to your breathing in the way we have just practised? And how often, on the other hand, do you just take it for granted, assuming that your body will keep you alive simply because that's what it has been doing all your life? Breathing is the most basic activity we engage in as living creatures. When we stop doing it for more than a few minutes, we die. And yet most of us rarely check in with this remarkable process – we rarely notice how it feels, on the most fundamental bodily level, to be alive.

If we hardly ever notice the texture, the quality, the fundamental feel of our breathing, something so very basic to our existence that we do it thousands of times every day

– then what else are we missing? What other experiences routinely pass us by, perhaps because we are busy thinking about the past or the future, or trying to get somewhere other than where we actually are? How much of our life do we live on automatic pilot?

We might discover a lot more about ourselves and about the world around us if we were able to pay more attention to the present moment, right here and now, in the same way that we just paid attention to our breathing. There is ordinary magic all around us: in the majesty of a tree, for example, perhaps one that has stood for hundreds of years, and whose living parts – leaves, branches, and trunk – are all as miraculous and mysterious as our own bodies. This magic is in other wonders of the natural world: the insects or rodents that crawl and scurry about beneath us, and in the stars and sun, those giant formations which nevertheless form only a tiny speck of a universe that we actually know so little about.

Perhaps we could pay more attention to man-made feats – sensing the ingredients in a delicious meal, really savouring their exquisite taste as we roll the food around our mouth with our tongue? Perhaps we could look up at the buildings in our street, and see how, brick upon brick, they have been carefully constructed, and how they shelter us from the elements? Or perhaps we could pay attention to the cursor on a computer screen, how it darts about when we shift an electronic mouse from side to side – how many of us really understand how and why this piece of technology works, or how it came to be invented?

AN ANCIENT PRACTICE

Paying attention to our world in this way – with mindfulness – has been recommended by wise men and women throughout history as a way of gaining a fresh, wider perspective, and turning us towards a saner way of life. The ancient Greek philosopher Socrates warned us to 'beware the barrenness of a busy life', declaring that 'wisdom begins in wonder' and even that 'the unexamined life is *not worth living*.'

Meditation has been a tool for opening up this wider perspective for a very long time. Human beings have been meditating as far back as records go – there are descriptions of yogic techniques in Hindu texts that were written around 2000–3000 BC. And they were probably practising well before that – it has been suggested that early men and women perhaps found themselves in a state of mindfulness when they gazed hypnotically at the flickering flames of a warm fire.

Meditation has appeared in virtually every culture across the world. Sometimes it has taken the form of religious practice, such as in Christianity, Judaism, Islam or shamanic rituals, and sometimes a secular healing discipline, such as in modern Western psychology. It has also been advocated as part of counter-cultural trends like the 20th-century 'hippie' and 'new age' movements. Whether for connecting with our spirituality or just calming down, meditation has, quietly, been everywhere – this fact alone suggests that people must have found it useful.

Even if you have never meditated, you have probably experienced moments in your life when you have felt really present to your body, to other people or to the environment – in the arms of a lover, perhaps, or standing by the sea. In these moments we feel connected, in touch with whatever it is we are experiencing, our body, mind and the world seeming naturally synchronised and in harmony. The psychologist Abraham Maslow called these moments 'peak experiences', and while they can happen naturally, when people start practising meditation they often begin to happen more often (although they can't be sought after!).

The root of the word 'meditation' is the Indo-European *med*, which means 'to measure'. By noticing something in a meditative way, we are both taking its measure and doing so in a measured way. We are watching something non-judgmentally, with awareness, aspiring to see it as it really is, rather than overlaid with the projections our minds habitually put onto the world.

A MANIFOLD PRACTICE

The word 'meditation' can refer to a wide range of practices. Some use concentration or visualisation, while others are based on contemplation and introspection. More still make use of physical movement, such as in martial arts or yoga – indeed, the Latin word *meditatio* originally meant *any* kind of exercise, physical or mental. Not all meditation practices are mindfulness meditations, but as most of them involve paying attention to an object of some kind they are likely to cultivate mindfulness.

The mindfulness practices we are exploring in this book – including the mindfulness of breathing exercise we have just been doing – are often associated with an Indian prince called Siddartha Gautama, who lived 2,500 years ago. Although born into great privilege, and despite his father showering him with luxury, Siddartha eventually realised that all the riches of the world couldn't save him, or anyone else, from the inevitable pains of human life – from the suffering associated with growing old, sickness and death, or with loss and unhappiness. Realising that there must be another way, he decided to leave the material comforts of his royal palace and instead pay attention to his mind, seeking liberation from the all-pervasive suffering that appeared to characterise human existence.

The story goes that, after studying with a number of teachers, and a further period of training in isolation, Siddhartha declared that he had found a way out of suffering. For the next 45 years, he taught his methods to those who also sought release from anguish. Siddhartha became known as the Buddha, which means the Awakened One, and his instructions on how to be more 'awake' included those on mindfulness. They have been passed down and practised by millions of people ever since.

THE FOUR NOBLE TRUTHS

Core to the Buddha's teaching were a set of principles he called The Four Noble Truths.[1] These four truths gave a concise diagnosis of the trials of human life, and a prescription for how they could be overcome.

THE FIRST NOBLE TRUTH

The Buddha's first truth seems obvious – that as human beings we experience suffering. We are born, we get ill, we die and, in between, our lives are punctuated by physical and mental pain of all kinds. Our bodies go wrong, wear out and eventually fall apart, and our minds are often in turmoil – we get angry, upset, frightened and depressed. No matter how rich we are, how well-toned our bodies, or how mentally balanced, we still experience a basic level of discomfort that seems to come simply with the fact of being human.

THE SECOND NOBLE TRUTH

The Buddha's second noble truth is that there is a root cause for all this suffering. We are troubled, said the Buddha, not so much because we are prey to the inconveniences of life, but because we constantly want *not* to experience them – we crave, cling to and chase after pleasure and we try to resist and escape pain. We don't want to have to face ageing, sickness and death, even though all three are inevitable. Unfortunately, by trying to hold on to pleasurable experiences, and trying to avoid painful ones, we cling to the way we *wish* things were, and resist how they *actually* are.

It is this clinging and avoidance that *really* create our suffering – what we are trying to achieve is impossible, and what we are trying to avoid is inevitable. All our efforts to change things which cannot be changed are futile, doomed to failure. In making all these efforts, we are out of step with the basic facts of life, jarring with reality – and it hurts. It is our desperate and impossible struggle to overturn the way things are that causes so much hardship, rather than the reality itself.

Even though we might think we know this on an intellectual level ('Of course I'm going to die, that's obvious!'), knowing it and accepting it are two different things – we resist these truths with our emotions and our behaviour. The explosion in cosmetic surgery is proof of this – in the UK, more than 34,000 invasive procedures are carried out each year – in the US it is over 12 million.[2] None of these expensive treatments will help us live longer, and they can only ever delay or mask the process of ageing. We may die wrinkle-free and smiling, with our faces in a state of permanent paralysis, but will we really be any happier? The more we try to deny the realities of our situation, the more suffering we tend to experience. But we just keep on struggling anyway – raging at life's insults, trying to run away from them, or taking elaborate steps to pretend they aren't happening. We are like animals trapped in a cage.

THE THIRD NOBLE TRUTH
But, said the Buddha, there is good news. His third noble truth is that there *is* a release from this predicament, and it comes in the form of a fourth truth, which he called the eightfold path.

THE FOURTH NOBLE TRUTH
The Buddha's eightfold path is a programme of intensive training, designed to realign our minds so that we can come into step with reality and move with the flow of life, rather than against it. The Buddha claimed that this means of training the mind would lead us away from grasping after

unattainable goals, and towards genuine liberation, which is to be found in a different way of seeing, and a different way of being. This path, as he laid it out 2,500 years ago, consists of:

- Right Understanding

- Right Thought

- Right Speech

- Right Action

- Right Livelihood

- Right Exertion

- Right Concentration

- Right Mindfulness.

The Buddha's contention was that by practising this path, one that leads to the cultivation of wise qualities in our minds and our lives, we can begin to live a more harmonious existence. Our minds can start to be in sync with the world as it is, in the present moment, rather than how we would like it to be, or to have been, in the future or the past.

In one memorable analogy, the Buddha said that our experience of suffering was a bit like being struck by two arrows. When we are hit with the first arrow, rather than thinking that this is painful enough, we voluntarily decide to shoot ourselves with another one! The first arrow is the unavoidable pain of our existence, and the second one is all the mental and emotional anguish we heap on top of it. We may have no choice about getting hit with the first arrow, but we *can* learn how to respond wisely to the pain it causes – we can learn *not to fire the second arrow*. We transform our experience by discovering how to relate to it differently. By working with our minds in this way, the Buddha maintained, we could actually reach a point where our suffering would stop completely.

RIGHT MINDFULNESS

As an element of the eightfold path, right mindfulness is a key part of the Buddha's training programme. If our minds remain untamed and speedy, we are likely to find that we often think, speak and act hastily, perhaps before we have even noticed what we are really doing. If the Buddha's students didn't cultivate right mindfulness, they would remain on the busy treadmill of overactivity, just as they always had done. They would keep acting impulsively, according to old patterns, even as they were trying to change.

In traditional descriptions, a busy mind is described as being like a host of wild animals. Sometimes it is a monkey, throwing itself agitatedly all over the place and chattering, and at others like a wild elephant, ploughing crazed through the jungle, leaving devastation in its wake. The point is the same: until our mind is stabilised, it is unlikely to do what we tell it to do.

The contemporary Buddhist teacher Sakyong Mipham Rinpoche says the mind is like a horse.[3] Through practising meditation we are neither fencing the horse in too tightly, nor letting it run wild. Gradually, through proper training,

we and the horse start to work together – the horse begins
to trust us, and we learn to ride.

By committing to the regular discipline of mindfulness
meditation, we can begin to tame our mind, training it
to see the world with discriminating awareness. Through
slowing down, doing less and noticing more, we too
can begin to see things more clearly, to see how habitual
patterns of thinking lead to suffering. We can begin to
understand which kinds of thoughts and actions result
in greater pain, and which result in greater wellbeing.
By training in mindfulness, we start to develop the
skill of refraining from unhelpful thoughts and actions,
and cultivating a lifestyle that is more in tune with the
natural order of things, and which could bring about real
contentment. From a Buddhist perspective, the application
of right mindfulness makes it more possible to develop the
other seven qualities on the eightfold path.

THE FOUR FOUNDATIONS OF MINDFULNESS

How, then, did the Buddha say this quality of mindfulness
could be cultivated? Fortunately, he gave some quite
straightforward advice on this point, most famously in a
teaching called The Four Foundations of Mindfulness. The
instructions contained in this teaching were considered
essential – the Buddha started his discourse by saying:
'This is the only way for the purification of beings, for the
overcoming of sorrow and lamentations, for the end of
suffering and grief, [and] for the attainment of the true
way.'[4]

He then goes on to describe four areas, or spheres, in which we can develop mindfulness. These four foundations of mindfulness relate to the body, the mind, our feelings, and everything that happens in our experience of daily life. He goes into each of these areas in some detail, but first he asks us to pay *particular* attention to our pattern of breathing, which he said is the primary means of developing all four foundations. He suggests going somewhere quiet ('the forest, the foot of a tree or an empty place') and sitting down with our 'legs crossed, body erect and mindfulness alert'. Then he gives instructions on how to engage in mindfulness meditation. Being 'ever mindful', the student 'breathes in, [and] mindful, he breathes out. Breathing in a long breath, he knows, "I am breathing in a long breath." Breathing out a long breath, he knows, "I am breathing out a long breath."'

It is a simple instruction, perhaps deceptively so. All the Buddha is suggesting is that we practise paying attention to our breathing, so that when we breathe, we really *know* what we are doing – not just intellectually, but with the entirety of our experience, body and mind, a bit like we did at the start of the chapter. Why not try it again now? Breathe in deeply and, as you do so, place your attention fully on your breath and nothing else – feel the sensation of the air in your nostrils, the rising of your chest, and the expansion of your abdomen. *Know* that you are 'breathing in a long breath'. Then, once you have inhaled fully, mindfully breathe out, placing your attention on the movement of the breath as it leaves your body. *Know* that you are breathing out a long breath.

The Buddha then continues with his description of how a student can breathe mindfully: 'Breathing in a short breath, he knows, "I am breathing in a short breath." Breathing out a short breath, he knows: "I am breathing out a short breath."'

How many times a day do you breathe like this, with full awareness, really *knowing*, at the deepest bodily level, what you are doing? And how many times a day do you breathe on automatic pilot, without really paying attention to what's going on at all? Do you think you could develop the ability to be conscious of a few more breaths each day? And if you took the time to notice your breathing in this way more often, what effect might it have on your speed and stress levels?

PRACTICE: Mindfulness of Breathing
To help you get started with a mindfulness of breathing practice, here are some more extended instructions ...

STEP ONE: BODY POSTURE
First, find a peaceful space where you won't be disturbed for a while. It could be your bedroom or, if your home is always busy, a quiet park. It is helpful to sit on something comfortable but firm, and which will support your body to stay upright. You can sit cross-legged on the floor, with cushions to support your bottom – a couple of telephone directories or similar-sized books under the cushions can help provide a steady base. Alternatively, you can sit on a chair or bench – however, if you do this try not to slump backwards, see if you can keep your spine straight and self-supporting (but not rigid), your legs uncrossed and

your feet flat on the ground. Lift your hands gently up onto your knees, or to wherever they land most comfortably in your lap. Keeping your eyes open, direct your gaze approximately 5 feet (1.5 metres) in front of you, towards the ground – there's no need to focus on any particular point, just keep your gaze soft. The posture should help you feel confident and relaxed. With your mouth slightly open, breathe naturally – just allow your breathing to settle.

STEP TWO: BREATH AWARENESS
Now, start to notice the movement of your breathing, in and out. There's no need to breathe particularly deeply or manipulate the breath in any way – just allow it to be as it naturally is. Let your body breathe for you – after all, that's what it's designed to do. Placing your attention gently on the breath, feel it enter through your nostrils. Notice its texture, and all the various sensations of breathing in your body – the filling of the abdomen, the rising and falling of the chest. Then feel the breath as it comes out and in through your nose and mouth. See if you can remain mindful of each complete breath, both inhaling and exhaling – perhaps sensing that you are gently synchronising your awareness with the movement of the breath, in and out. There's no need to concentrate too hard – your attention can be gentle and light. At the same time, you are not particularly trying to relax. Just allow yourself to be with your breathing, and with your experience, however it is.

STEP THREE: WORKING WITH THOUGHTS
As you practise like this, you will notice thoughts, feelings and bodily sensations arise. This is normal – thinking and

feeling are part of being alive. However, while you are meditating, see if you can allow those thoughts, feelings and bodily sensations just to pass through, without either holding on to them or shutting them out. Just be aware of them, and let them go. It's a bit like standing on the bank of a river, watching objects passing by. There could be objects we're interested in (fish, leaves, the branch of a tree) or, if the river is dirty, objects we're revolted by – dirty plastic bottles, used condoms or sewage. Normally we might become engrossed in the flow of objects, telling ourselves stories about where they've come from. We might be either attracted to them or repulsed by them, and follow them to see where they go next. But in this meditation, we are simply noticing all the flotsam and jetsam of thoughts and feelings passing through our mind and body, sometimes flowing as a trickle, sometimes a torrent. Instead of identifying with and following our thoughts, we let them pass through, continuing to place our awareness lightly and gently on the breath.

Before long, you will probably notice that your mind has wandered from awareness on the breath. Perhaps it has started planning what you will have for dinner, or is going over a conversation you had earlier on in the day. That's fine, it is not a problem or a mistake, it's just what the mind does. When you notice your mind has wandered away from the breath, just acknowledge that briefly, and then bring it gently back. Do this without judgement or criticism – it is simply part of the process of meditation. Now, return to a light and gentle awareness of your breath, as it moves naturally, in and out.

Soon, your mind will wander again – maybe you're telling yourself a story about an emotion you are feeling – anger, sadness, excitement – or your mind is just drifting around aimlessly. Once again, when you notice that your mind has wandered away from the breath, just acknowledge that (perhaps saying to yourself, 'Aha, mind wandering', if you find it helps), and then gently return to a light and gentle attention on the breath. Each time you notice your mind has wandered, gently and kindly acknowledge it, and then return to the breath as it moves naturally, in and out of your body.

Keep repeating this process – coming back to the breath again and again – for the period of time you have decided to practise.

WHY PAY ATTENTION TO THE BREATH?

THE BREATH IS FUNDAMENTAL TO OUR 'BEING'
In mindfulness, we are cultivating our ability to *be with* our direct experience – we are not thinking about what we're doing, or creating a story about it, but actually embodying it, right now, as it happens. When we pay attention to the breath, we are disengaging temporarily from thinking and doing, and engaging with life on its most essential, basic, level – awareness of our breathing shifts us naturally towards a simple and deep experience of being. Paying attention to our breathing, the very rhythm of existence, is a simple way to appreciate the magic of being alive.

OUR BREATH IS ALWAYS AVAILABLE

If we are alive, we are breathing. By training to be mindful of the breath, we are becoming familiar with a simple tool that can always be used as a steadying anchor to bring us into awareness, wherever we happen to be. When our mind is darting about all over the place, we can practise directing our attention to our breathing. By doing this again and again, we are training our minds to be more stable, centred and calm.

WE DON'T NEED TO CONTROL THE BREATH

It is part of us, but we don't need to manipulate our breathing in any way. That the breath operates without us having to *do* anything reminds us that underneath everything, we can just *be* – we don't always need to be rushing around, chasing goals, forcing our experience or constantly analysing everything. We can just allow our present experience to *be* there – we can accept it and observe it. Paying attention to the breath is therefore a practical exercise in developing a more mindful relationship to our lives. It reminds us that, at our deepest level, we already know how to be.

After showing his students how to breathe mindfully, the Buddha then gave them a number of instructions on being mindful of the body. These include reminders on physical posture (the student 'knows, when he is standing "I am standing" … he knows, when he is lying down, "I am lying down"'), how to perform daily activities ('in bending and stretching, he applies clear comprehension, in eating, drinking, chewing and savouring, he applies clear comprehension ... in walking, in standing, in sitting, in falling asleep, in waking, in speaking and in keeping silence, he applies clear comprehension.'). Again, the point is clear: in each of our activities, as we go about our lives, the key to mindfulness is to really *be with* whatever we are doing, so that we are living consciously and wakefully, rather than on automatic pilot.

Then the Buddha turns to the other three foundations of mindfulness – our mind, feelings and everything else that happens in our experience of daily life, making the same point with regard to each: we can use every aspect of our lives to train in mindfulness. So, the instruction applies to the mind: he 'knows the distracted state of consciousness as the distracted state of consciousness ... the concentrated state of consciousness as the concentrated state', and to feelings: a student, 'when experiencing a pleasant feeling, knows, "I experience a pleasant feeling"; when experiencing a painful feeling, he knows, "I experience a painful feeling."' And it applies to how we think, feel and behave in every aspect of our lives – when we are doing our jobs, perhaps, enjoying time with our friends and family, going shopping, or even watching television.

The Buddha encourages us to be mindful of how we experience his Four Noble Truths – how we suffer, how our clinging leads to suffering, and how the elements of the eightfold path lead us towards freedom. For Buddhists, being mindful here doesn't mean agreeing to believe these truths on faith alone, or learning them as if they were a creed or catechism – it means really investigating them through personal experience, examining for themselves whether what the Buddha said makes sense. Finally, perhaps because so many of us have a tendency to focus solely on the difficult experiences of life, we are reminded also to notice some of the signs of our developing wellbeing – our energy, joy, tranquillity, concentration and equanimity. And, in case we haven't yet got the message, we are even invited to take notice of our mindfulness – to be mindful of how mindful we are being!

The advice, then, is clear. If we want to suffer less, we must pay mindful attention to our lives. We can start by being mindful of our breathing – the most fundamental of all our bodily experiences – and then expand that outwards to the whole of the body. We can pay attention to our feelings, and see how we grasp on to pleasant experiences, and how we try to avoid unpleasant ones. And we can notice how grasping and avoidance create problems in our mind, and how we then project those problems out into our life.

With mindfulness, we can begin to *observe* our experience at the same time as participating in it, to really *know* what we are doing, when we are doing it. By watching ourselves and our lives in this way, we can begin to get a better sense of how we operate in the world, and be able to notice more often when what we think and do leads to suffering. We can start to get a better insight into what makes for a genuinely happy life and, as we develop our powers of mindfulness, we can start to choose consciously to act in new, healthier ways. Rather than busily and mindlessly rushing through our lives, we can train in paying mindful attention – we can wake up!

THE BUDDHA AND PSYCHOLOGY

Mindfulness isn't some religious concept, and it isn't necessary to become a Buddhist to benefit from practising it. The Buddha was sharing a practical realisation, based on his own experience, of how to live a less stressful, healthier existence. Mindfulness is certainly deeply rooted in the Buddhist tradition, but it doesn't exclusively belong to it. If what the Buddha said about the importance of being mindful is true, then it was inevitable that this would be discovered and corroborated by other people, at different times in history, using the methods of their time. And that is what has started to happen in the discipline of Western psychology.

With its focus on using experimental methods to try to discover the truth about the human mind, Western psychology has much in common with Buddhism. If he were alive today, the Buddha might well be considered a psychologist rather than a religious leader, and his practice instructions would probably be considered a kind of psychotherapy. Even his attitude has echoes in modern science – although Buddhism is sometimes thought of as a religion, the Buddhist approach is quite unlike what we often think of in the West as being religious. Rather than asking his students to take what he said at face value, the Buddha said that confidence in his eightfold path had to come from people's own experience of testing it out. Rather than saying: 'Believe what I say is true and everything will be fine,' he said, 'Why not try it out for yourself and see what happens?' The instructions are based on life in the here and now, and he encouraged people to approach them with an attitude of healthy scepticism. Like a scientific researcher, he invited students to use their own minds as a laboratory.

William James, one of the founding fathers of Western psychology, could have been talking about mindfulness when he wrote that, 'The faculty of voluntarily bringing back a wandering attention, over and over again, is the very root of judgement, character and will. No one is master of himself if he have it not.'[5] Unfortunately, James was less confident about how this faculty might be developed, lamenting that 'it is easier to define this ideal than to give practical directions for bringing it about.' Unlike the Buddha's students, it seems that James did not have the benefit of knowing how to practise mindfulness meditation.

Sigmund Freud was also onto something mindful when he recommended that psychoanalysts should aim to keep a 'calm, quiet attentiveness [and] evenly-hovering attention'[6] when they were seeing patients. Many of Freud's ideas sound like echoes of Buddhist teachings – like the Buddha, Freud suggested that our present experience is affected by patterns of thinking, perceiving, feeling and behaving that have been set in the past, and, like the Buddha, he suggested that the way to a happier existence is to bring those patterns to light – that through being more conscious of them, we might be able to make more appropriate, enlightened responses.

Also like the Buddha, Freud realised that it would take more than just insight for people to really change their behaviour (he apparently once said that giving a patient insight into their condition was like giving a starving person a menu).

As Western psychology blossomed during the 20th century, more of its great practitioners had ideas which bear similarities to Buddhist teachings. In the 1950s, Albert Ellis suggested that mental illnesses such as depression arise not so much as a result of what happens to us in our lives, as how we interpret those events in our minds. Realising that if you could change the content of people's thoughts you might then relieve some of their emotional distress, Ellis developed a new form of treatment called 'Rational Emotive Behaviour Therapy' (REBT), designed to help patients challenge existing, unhelpful ways of thinking which, he felt, contributed to mental illness.[7] With its intention to relieve suffering by changing our minds, the framework behind REBT sounds not so different to the Four Noble Truths. Wasn't it the Buddha who first said: 'With our thoughts we make the world'?[8]

It was only a matter of time before psychologists and scientists began not only to echo the theory of what the Buddha taught about suffering, but to test out the practices he prescribed as treatment.

RESEARCH INTO MEDITATION

There had already been a smattering of scientific studies on meditation in the 1930s, 1940s and 1950s, but the

work really began in earnest in the 1960s. The first pieces
of research mostly reported its effects on the body's
metabolism – consumption of oxygen, body temperature
and heart and breathing rate. Then, in the 1970s,
researchers such as Herbert Benson and Robert Wallace
found that meditation encourages health-promoting
changes in the body's self-regulation mechanisms,
including blood pressure and heart rate. [9] This was the first
real scientific proof of what millions of meditators had
discovered over the centuries: that meditation can help
relieve stress and bring physical health benefits.

By the 1990s, researchers into meditation were looking not
only at the short-term effects that the practices might have
on the body – a temporary lowering of blood pressure, or a
slower heart rate – but whether meditation might actually
induce more long-term changes, even in the brain. After all,
the promise of the Buddha was that by following the path
of meditation, our experience might start to be transformed
not just during formal practice, but in every aspect of
our lives. This would mean not just that we had achieved
some fleeting state of calm – a result, perhaps, of sitting
somewhere quiet and not doing very much – but that
really deep change was occurring in our minds, sufficient
to alter, fundamentally, our experience of the world we live
in. If that were the case, might there not be some physical
evidence of this transformation, some way we could
actually see the mark of practice in our brains?

Until recently this would have been considered a strange idea
in scientific circles. Of course, it was widely accepted that the
condition of our brains has a big influence on how our minds

experience the world – for instance, if you were involved in a car accident or suffered a stroke, causing damage to the brain, it might well affect your ability to think or perform certain actions which would previously have been easy for you. However, the possibility that this could work the other way around – that we might be able to affect the make-up of the brain by how we use our minds – seemed pretty unlikely. It used to be thought that the function of specific nerve cells in the brain was firmly fixed by adulthood – while there was considerable change and growth in the brain during childhood, once you became an adult you were basically stuck with the brain you already had.

However, thanks to new technology which enables researchers to look closely at the structure and functioning of the human brain, scientists have realised that this is not quite the case. Researchers can now look in much more detail at the activity of our brains and can get a clearer picture than ever before of how we use them. Techniques such as electro-encephalography allow us to study electrical activity in the brain, while Functional Magnetic Resonance Imaging (fMRI) lets us look in great detail at which parts of the brain are most active when we're carrying out certain functions. Information and images from these studies have allowed neuroscientists to discover and map which regions of the brain 'light up' when we learn a new language, solve a maths problem or think about someone we know.

BRAIN CHANGE

This technology has taught us a lot about how the brain works, and we now know that structural changes in the brain can and do occur throughout our lifetime – not only are fresh connections made between neurons, but new neurons are created – around 5,000 a day! Thanks to modern brain scans, neuroscientists have shown that these brain changes are affected by what we do in our lives – a phenomenon that has been called *neuroplasticity*.

For example, by scanning the brains of London taxi drivers, it has been discovered that, on average, cabbies have a larger hippocampus than the rest of us.[10] The hippocampus is a part of the brain associated with spatial processing and memory, a quality that taxi drivers might be expected to exercise regularly, given that they have to navigate complex street configurations as they ferry people around a large, sprawling city. Could it be that London taxi drivers have larger hippocampi because they have to carry out intensive memorisation exercises when they train to do their job, and then continue to use that part of the brain regularly whenever they are at work?

It seems highly likely that it is the taxi driver's job that makes the difference to his or her brain – researchers have found that the hippocampi of cabbies who have been doing the job for longer are larger than those of newly-qualified drivers. Similarly, people who speak several languages have enlarged areas of the brain that relate to word processing,[11] whilst the brains of musicians who play stringed instruments are different in the areas that relate to fine motor movement.[12]

The phenomenon of neuroplasticity seems to work in the same way as body conditioning. Nobody seems very surprised that lifting heavy weights can make the muscles in your arms grow stronger, so is it really that surprising that engaging in mental exercise trains the brain in the same way? Perhaps not, but until the phenomenon of neuroplasticity became detectable through technology, there was no evidence that this might be the case. The fact that we now have such evidence has big ramifications – it suggests that qualities of mind such as attention, empathy, or even joy, can be developed in exactly the same way as the muscles in our bodies. As the Buddha suggested, we may be able to train ourselves to be wiser and more content.

This goes directly counter to what neuroscientists and psychologists used to think. It had been thought that personality attributes such as happiness were basically fixed, at least once we'd reached adulthood. While we all know that our day-to-day experience of wellbeing goes up and down, fluctuating according to what we are doing and what happens to us, it had been thought that once we reached adulthood we had a fairly stable 'happiness set-point'.[13] Even if something really wonderful or really awful happened to us, once the initial surprise or shock was over, before long we would return pretty much to the level of contentment we experienced prior to the apparently life-changing event.

So it was seen that when people win the lottery, for instance, their mood would go up for a while, but within a year or two they were usually about as happy or unhappy as they were before they received their windfall.[14] Similarly, when someone had an accident that left them in a wheelchair, they felt more miserable than usual for a while, but after that they too returned to their usual mood range.

Of course, this range is different for each of us – some people are generally cheerful, a few of us are mostly miserable, and the rest are somewhere in between. But wherever we were on the scale, it had been assumed that this was largely inherent, a mainly innate property of our personalities.

Our personalities *are* hard to change. Just as all the weight training in the world won't turn an 8-stone guy into a heavyweight boxing champion, so we *do* have predispositions towards particular qualities of character. However, the phenomenon of neuroplasticity suggests that our personalities may not be as irrevocably determined as had previously been believed.

These findings map uncannily closely the teachings given by the Buddha. Buddhist psychology says that patterns of thinking, feeling and behaviour are deeply ingrained. But it also says that we have the power to change these patterns. Neuroplasticity seems to suggest the same: that while our genes and the physical structure of our brains are powerful determinants of our experience, the fact that we can change our brains by what we do with our minds gives us significant potential for altering what might have seemed to be our 'destiny'. By training ourselves to think and act differently, we can potentially begin to free ourselves from patterns that appeared to be fixed, even within the structure of our brains.

THE NEUROSCIENCE OF MEDITATION

The question, then, is what kind of training does the mind need in order to change in ways that will be beneficial? What can we do to become happier, not just as a short-term pleasure hit, but over the long haul? The Buddha's contention was that one of the primary ways to become more genuinely happy was to engage in the practice of mindfulness. And, while the field of neuroplasticity is still really only taking its first baby steps, the early evidence it is producing seems to back up what the Buddha said.

At the Laboratory for Affective Neuroscience at the University of Wisconsin, Professor Richard Davidson has been investigating the neuroscience of meditation and wellbeing for the best part of two decades.[15] His research suggests not only that significant brain changes occur as a result of practising meditation, but that these changes are associated with the development of a greater sense of wellbeing.

First of all, Davidson found a way to tell how content a person generally is by analysing the electrical activity in the person's brain, using EEG readings. He took hundreds of readings from different people, and found that when they are upset, anxious, angry or depressed, they tend to exhibit more activity in certain parts of the brain – most notably the area around the amygdala, which is sometimes known as the brain's 'fear centre', and also an area called the right prefrontal cortex, which is located just behind the forehead.[16] He also found that when people are feeling more upbeat, there is more activity in the *left* prefrontal cortex, and less happening in the amygdala and right prefrontal cortex.

Davidson has found that he can use his readings to predict people's basic mood tendencies – the more activity they generally show on the right, the likelier they are to have a gloomy outlook, while the more activity they show on the left, the more content a person tends to be. Those who show most extreme activity on the right are more likely to have experienced clinical depression or an anxiety disorder at some point in their lives.

All this seems to support the idea of a fixed happiness set-point. But what happens if someone engages in a regime of mindfulness meditation? If the Buddha was right, then training in mindfulness might be able to alter that set-point, to help people become happier – not just when something pleasurable happens to them, but at a deeper, longer-lasting level. Could such training actually make a difference to people's minds? And if so, might there be some trace of that change visible in the brain?

In an experiment designed to find out, Davidson took readings from a group of office workers at a company called Promega in Madison, Wisconsin.[17] He did this both before and after they'd taken a weekly, two-month course in mindfulness meditation. The workers were stressed, and before the course their brain readings suggested that, on average, they were at the more unhappy end of the scale – there was more activity than average in the right prefrontal cortex of their brains. Following the mindfulness training, however, not only did the workers report feeling more positive, more energetic, more engaged in their work and less stressed, but the readings from their brains had changed as well: there was more activity in their left prefrontal cortexes than before, and less activity on the right. The subjects were tested again after another four months – remarkably, the changes had been sustained. This was significant – it suggested that learning how to be mindful, even over just a couple of months, had made a lasting imprint.

Dr Sara Lazar is another neuroscientist who has studied the impact of meditation on the brain. She used MRI scans to look at the brains of people who had practised mindfulness for many years, and compared them with people who had no meditation experience. The results showed that in the meditators, areas of the brain cortex associated with attention and sensory processing were thicker than in the non-meditators, with the difference in cortical thickness greatest in those subjects who had been meditating the longest.[18] The findings are preliminary, but the results seem to suggest that mental training in mindfulness might have actually bulked up the meditators' brains, just as a programme of physical training can bulk up the muscles of the body. Another study by a group of researchers at UCLA also found that meditators had more grey matter in areas of the brain linked to regulating the emotions; these areas included the hippocampus, the orbito-frontal cortex, the thalamus and the inferior temporal lobe.[19]

Thanks to neuroscience, then, we are beginning to accumulate hard material evidence for what the Buddha was suggesting all those centuries ago, and what meditators following in his footsteps have been saying ever since: taking 'mental exercise', in the form of meditation, can benefit wellbeing in exactly the same way as taking physical exercise. Just as we are all now used to being told how we can make significant differences to our health if we take care of our bodies – eating well, getting plenty of exercise and sleep – so we might be able to make a similarly positive difference to our health by training our minds. Our psychological wellbeing is not entirely limited by our genes or our upbringing. By practising mindfulness, we can train to become happier.

Over the next four chapters we will be looking further at how mindfulness can be used to help us cope with a range of 21st-century challenges, and how the original mindful manifesto, the Buddha's Four Foundations of Mindfulness, are just as relevant for observing and working with our bodies, feelings, minds and life experiences today as they were 2,500 years ago.

You don't have to become a Buddhist to benefit from this mental exercise, nor do you have to sign up to any particular 'religious' belief – mindfulness is not something to believe in, it is something to do. Of course, you do need to be open-minded enough to give it a try in the first place, and to stick with it if it isn't always easy. Ultimately, confidence in mindfulness should come, not from the Buddha, not from neuroscientists, and certainly not from this book – if it comes, it should come from the fruit of your own experience.

Before you move on to the next chapter, we'd like to invite you to return to the mindful breathing practice (page

45) and go through each step again, to start familiarising yourself with it. It's worth remembering that mindfulness *is* just that – a practice. Knowing the theory alone won't make much difference. It's a bit like learning how to play a musical instrument – you can only develop proficiency by doing it regularly. Reading books about how to play a musical instrument won't allow you to master the violin, and so it is with mindfulness meditation – reading about it might supply you with motivation and a conceptual framework, but until you commit to regular practice, you can't really expect much to happen.

MINDFULNESS OF BREATHING: SUGGESTIONS FOR GETTING STARTED

SCHEDULING PRACTICE
Some people are better able to meditate in the morning, when their minds are fresh. Others prefer the evening, when they are more able to let go of the day's pressures. Experiment with what works best for you. Whatever you decide, see if you can stay with it, so that your practice becomes a good habit, a bit like brushing your teeth.

TIMING SESSIONS
Setting an alarm clock at the start of your practice makes a clear intention for how long you are going to meditate, and means your mind can let go of thinking about how much time is left before you stop.

PACING YOURSELF
Short, regular sessions tend to be the best way to start, rather than longer or more infrequent practice. It's better to

sit for 5 or 10 minutes than plan to meditate for an hour but never get round to it because it's too daunting, or because you feel you don't have enough time. Developing a practice is a bit like starting physical exercise – you wouldn't try to complete a marathon before training your body with regular, shorter runs.

DON'T WAIT FOR CONDITIONS TO BE PERFECT

It's helpful to have a quiet place to meditate, and to feel ready and motivated before you begin. But if there are distractions, then you can just notice and accept them as you would notice your thoughts. Even if you don't feel in the mood to start – see if you can just do it anyway.

DROPPING PRECONCEPTIONS

'Meditation is religious ... meditation is done by hippies or new-age weirdos ... meditation is too hard for me ... I'm too stressed out to meditate ... I'm going to *love* meditating.' Whatever ideas you might have, see if you can let them go and approach the practice with a fresh mind. Imagine you were being asked to try something you had never heard of before – wouldn't you be curious as to what might happen?

STAYING WITH IT

Our overactive minds love having new toys to play with – including meditation practices! If we try lots of different techniques at once, we run the risk of using meditation as yet another way to keep our minds busy. Rather than racing ahead to the exercises in later chapters, see if you can practise mindful breathing every day, for 10 minutes a day, for a week. In this way, your mind can start to become familiar with it – one Tibetan word for meditation (*gom*) actually means 'becoming familiar'. Remember, some meditators fruitfully practise *just* mindfulness of breathing for their whole lives.

TESSA'S EXPERIENCE

Tessa has been practising mindfulness in the Buddhist tradition for 17 years – meditation has helped her to deal with stress and eczema, as well as giving her the ability to really appreciate life.

Tessa first became interested in meditation in 1992, when she was going through a particularly tough time at work. 'I was a trainee radio producer,' she remembers, 'working on a live daily programme. I was learning the ropes so I was quite stressed out. I had always suffered from eczema, but it was really bad at that point – my skin was red, inflamed and itchy.'

Having booked herself a holiday in Corsica, Tessa spotted a book on meditation at the airport. Wondering if it might help with her stress, she took it away with her. 'I sat under a fig tree in the shade, and started to follow the instructions. I was looking for some sort of calm and peacefulness, and it gave me a glimpse of that.'

Back home, she started to look at how she might develop her practice further. 'I was invited by a friend to the London Shambhala Meditation Centre, which is a Buddhist centre but with a tradition of presenting meditation as something that anyone can do, without having to be a Buddhist.'

Although at first Tessa was just looking for stress relief, she discovered something more. 'After a while, I did a full weekend of meditation, and that was when it really clicked for me. I discovered that the practice had something very profound to it, which I'd describe as an experience of much greater spaciousness, of the world being really vivid. I felt like I was stepping outside of the thought patterns that were trapping me, and feeling like there was a much bigger world out there.'

Although initially wary of anything that seemed too religious, Tessa began to take an interest in the origins of the practices she was being taught. 'I began to trust the Buddhist tradition, because everything that I was being told resonated with what I was discovering for myself. That encouraged me to investigate more, and slowly I became more interested in the kind of perspective it offers. It felt like something that could transform me as a person, although at the same time I was also settling into an acceptance of who I was, and not having to struggle so much to be something different.'

Tessa attributes many of the positive changes she has experienced over the years to her meditation practice. 'I am quite a speedy person, and before I started meditating I missed 99 per cent of what was happening in my day. I didn't even taste the food I was eating. I can be very caught up in all kinds of busy-ness, but through the practice we learn to let go of our thoughts and the habitual patterns that we are so addicted to. We are training in watching our mind and seeing how busy it is, and then dropping that. Because I am practising, I am much more able to notice when I am walking down a street and there is a lovely tree in front of me. I can wake up to where I am in the present moment and really appreciate what is going on. I am less trapped in thoughts about the past, or worries about the future. I feel more alive and awake to my own experience, and more accepting of it, rather than wishing things were different. That brings a sense of joy.'

Tessa also says that meditation has enabled her to respond more attentively when she is under pressure. 'I am less reactive – I don't throw a temper tantrum or lash out at people as much as I used to. There are certainly still times when I feel my temper, but I am more able to feel the thoughts and emotions that might be whirring around and causing me to react, and then be able to make a choice about the way I deal with that. I might still feel stress, but I don't *buy into* it as much. There is a sense of it happening in a bigger space, of not believing in it so strongly and of just observing it. I am less likely to accelerate the stress by adding to it myself!'

Meditation also seems to have had a tangible impact on Tessa's eczema. 'The difference is really noticeable – it's hardly there any more. It's gone from being a really difficult physical challenge to being very mild and under control.'

Over the years of practice, Tessa has noticed how her mindfulness seems to relate directly to how much she practises meditation. 'I have had periods where I have practised very regularly, and periods where I haven't,' she says, 'and I can always really feel the difference. When I am practising for 10, 20 or 30 minutes in the morning, that has a huge impact on whether I'm able to be more mindful during the rest of the day.'

Jonty's Experience

I would like to say that I manage to meditate regularly, but I don't. Like so many aspirations I have, what I know in theory is hard to translate into practice. Practising being mindful of my breathing is so simple, and I am aware that the effects on my life can be profound. Yet somehow I still struggle with it – as with many other things in my life, I tend to look for quick results.

For a long time I imagined that I was just busier than everybody else, or that my mind was harder to work with than most. I used to look at other people as they sat and meditated and I would imagine their clear tranquil minds, whilst inside mine it felt like a storm was raging! Thankfully, much of the training I had involved discussion groups where we could share our experiences, and during these I started to I realise that I was not alone – other people were having the same difficulties as me, with physical aches and pains and wild minds that sometimes felt like they would never settle. Learning about meditation and mindfulness in a structured way like this was incredibly helpful to me. Sharing my experience with others gave me confidence and support.

As time has gone on I have started to notice my breath more often, and now I quite naturally place my mind on my breath when I want to relax. As soon as I do this, I become aware of my busy head, all the thoughts bouncing around – energised by whatever emotion happens to be driving them at that moment. Within a few seconds I am usually carried off by them and have to remind myself, once again, to come back to my breath. The stronger the emotion, the harder it is to let go, and even when I try I will often go back to the same thoughts again and again – reliving an argument, finding flaws in another person's case and strengthening my own, or daydreaming about my next holiday. Through all this my breath acts like an anchor. Sometimes when my mind is particularly stormy it feels as though it won't hold and I fall back on all my usual techniques for managing my anxiety by getting busy; with practice, though, my confidence in my breath, my body and my mind has grown and I know now that, at some level, I can work with any situation without drowning.

Ed's Experience

My mind has always had a tendency to work fast. Sometimes this has served me well – at school and university, my quick intellect got me good grades and praise from teachers. As a journalist, being able to turn my thoughts into words at speed was a crucial part of doing my job well. But a fast-paced mind has drawbacks: sometimes I am too caught up in my thoughts to notice what's going on around me – I miss the experience of actually being in the moment, of really living life. When there's too much going on in my head, I start to feel overwhelmed – and rather than slowing down I tend to speed up even more, trying to find an intellectual solution to what is actually a problem caused by over-intellectualisation.

Mindfulness meditation – simply taking the time and space to connect with experience through paying attention to the breath – is a simple antidote to my speed. I won't pretend that years of practice have eliminated my habitual tendency towards going too fast – they haven't. But meditation has given me a glimpse of what it is like to balance 'doing' with 'being' – to relax into experience, rather than always trying to control it. Mindfulness is a literal breathing space – and it gives me a choice, where previously I felt I had none. Sometimes this can be frustrating – the pull to deal with problems by trying to solve rather than letting go of them can be strong. When I am being mindful, it can feel as if I am doing precisely the opposite of what I 'should'. Equally, it can be a surprise to find that I start to feel better once I relinquish control of what's happening and simply pay attention to it.

Buddhist teachings tell us that these patterns are built up over many lifetimes, and are not easily changed – whether that be true or not, I take it as permission to be less than perfect, to relax as much as I can, and just to do my best. I don't have to get it all sorted today, this week, or even in this lifetime. Probably I am still less mindful than some people who have never meditated, but I see it very much like physical exercise – we all start at different levels of fitness, and our minds, as well as our bodies, have different capabilities. I may not always be very mindful, but I am certainly more mindful than I was 10 years ago.

CHAPTER THREE

MINDFULNESS OF BODY

Practise being mindful of your body – reconnecting mind and body can help us experience the wholeness of being, as well as preventing and treating physical illness.

Imagine, for a moment, a situation that's guaranteed to make you stressed. Perhaps you're in a school hall, about to sit the most important exam of your life – one that will decide your future – and your mind has gone blank. You can't answer any of the questions on the paper, and you're convinced you're going to fail. Or maybe you're in an aeroplane that has unexpectedly hit turbulence – all of a sudden the wings start shuddering, you are shunted from side to side, and there's an instantaneous drop in altitude – it feels like you're falling out of the sky. Or it could be that you've made a big mistake at work – one that's going to cost your company a lot of money. Your boss has found out, and you've been summoned to her office. You're sure you're going to get fired.

Whatever situation you choose, see if you can visualise it so that it feels real, that it's really happening. As you transport yourself into this stressful state, what happens in your body? Are your palms starting to sweat? Has your mouth gone dry? Have you got butterflies in your stomach? Is your jaw tense? Do you feel the effect of putting your mind's attention on this scenario in your body?

Now imagine how much more powerful these sensations might be if you really did find yourself in that stressful place right now? Perhaps you might get palpitations, or feel a sudden need to go to the toilet.

It only takes a simple exercise like this to realise that our minds and bodies are intimately connected – that when we experience stress in our minds, it has a corresponding effect in our bodies.

THE MIND–BODY CONNECTION

Unfortunately, when it comes to looking after our health, we often behave as though this mind–body connection isn't there at all. When we get ill, most of us get hooked on our physical aches and pains – we hardly ever recognise the vital role that psychological wellbeing plays, in both making us ill and in getting us well again. We often treat a visit to our GP or the hospital like a trip to the garage for our car – we expect the doctor or nurse to ask a few questions, do some tests, tell us what is wrong and then repair it. But it isn't that simple.

Doctors can take some responsibility for this. Medical training breeds a mechanical kind of healthcare – the human 'machine' is broken down into all its material components, and the job of the physician is to try to work out where in the body the problem is. Then they try either to fix or replace the faulty part. Medicine has developed this way of working because it's based on scientific method, which relies on detailed observation and experimentation to find out how things work. In many respects this is a great way of doing things, but it has its drawbacks. It means we place far greater importance on what we can see than what we can't, focusing in on material detail rather than zooming out to the bigger picture.

Modern medicine has dissected the human body into smaller and smaller parts – we can examine it under microscopes that magnify the tiniest bits of us to two million times their size. When something in our body bothers us, we go and see the expert for that area: the cardiologist, the neurologist, the gastroenterologist – every part of us has a corresponding specialist.

The danger of this approach is that we lose sight of the fact that we aren't just made up of biology and chemistry – the parts that are visible on an X-ray or that show up on a blood test. We are also our minds: a matrix of emotions, thoughts, personality, relationships and beliefs, and these are elements that you can't home in on with a scanner, or prod with a scalpel.

Taken to its extreme, our conventional model of health doesn't really recognise that we have minds at all – you will sometimes still hear medical students talking to each other about 'that amazing heart murmur in bed 14' or 'the liver cancer in bed 22'. Patients become their diagnosis – a collection of disconnected flesh and bones, rather than a whole person made up of many interconnected parts.

Whether we recognise it or not, our minds have an impact on how we experience health. It has been shown again and again in research that our mood affects when and how we get sick, as well as our prospects for recovery. People prone to mental illness are at a much higher risk of a whole range of other health problems, including cardiovascular disease and diabetes.[1] When someone takes a positive attitude to illness, he or she generally fares better than those who are overwhelmed by their condition.

Connecting body and mind is especially important when we face an illness that medicine has no simple answer to. Despite all our amazing technology, we still don't have cures for many of the most common health problems that trouble us. Heart disease, high blood pressure, asthma, arthritis – medicine can help us manage conditions like these, but in most cases there is no way to make them go away.

Virtually all of us, at some time in our lives, will have to learn to live with chronic illness. And when we do, our state of mind will have a big impact on how we cope with our situation.

Unfortunately, by acting as if our bodies are machines, we often make things worse. When some people get sick, they focus so hard on fixing their body that they put themselves into a state of struggle. They long for things to be different from how they are, or they fight to try and find a cure. Surely the doctor can order some more tests, or send them for a second opinion? Perhaps another doctor will be able to make a diagnosis and select a treatment that the GP has missed? There must be a tablet, an injection, or an operation that can make the body work again. After all, if they can clone sheep, surely they must be able to work out what's causing *my* pain?

Working out what's wrong with us isn't always that easy. Many aches and pains don't fit into neat diagnostic categorisations – they can't be always be seen, understood, classified or rectified just by looking at an X-ray or by going under the surgeon's knife. Some 20 per cent of adults suffer from chronic pain,[2] and much of it can't be pinpointed to a visible cause in the body. In around a third of all GP consultations in the UK, the symptoms a patient comes in with will remain unexplained by the time they leave.[3]

Struggling to fight an illness that has no cure doesn't usually work – it starts to take up an even larger slice of our time, attention and energy, which only makes the pain loom larger. And it creates stress. We know that stress is a contributor to and factor in many chronic illnesses: cardio-vascular disease, diabetes, high blood pressure, irritable bowel and chronic fatigue syndromes, as well as a number of skin complaints. Stress puts strain on our heart, raises our pulse and blood pressure, suppresses our immune system, disturbs the digestive system and sends our blood sugar levels up. It can also give us headaches and migraines, as well as disturbing our sleep – insomnia then makes our body even weaker. When we get stressed in the search to find a cure for being ill, it's a strategy that often backfires – a classic example of firing the second arrow of suffering on top of the first arrow of pain, of using the overactive mode to tackle a problem that can't be solved by more and more doing.

STRESS AND THE AUTONOMIC NERVOUS SYSTEM

The autonomic nervous system helps our body to function. It keeps our heart beating, our bowels moving and our lungs breathing automatically, through a complex system of chemical and electrical signals. It's sensitive to the smallest changes in our body – even the simple act of standing up is accompanied by an automatic adjustment in our arteries and heart rate, so we don't faint from the change in blood pressure. The autonomic nervous system also senses variations in our environment – helping our bodies respond to changing light levels or temperature.

It stays alert for any sign of danger that might threaten us, preparing us instinctively to fight or run away. In our evolutionary history, this 'fight or flight' response helped us survive as a species – like most other animals, we had to react instantaneously to the movement of predators that wanted to kill us.

A part of the autonomic nervous system, called the 'sympathetic' nervous system, responds to threats by releasing adrenaline. This diverts resources to parts of the body which need to step up a gear – it speeds up our heart rate, takes blood from our gut to our muscles, dilates our pupils to allow more light into the eyes, and opens up the airways in our lungs to increase the flow of oxygen. It also releases cortisol, a natural steroid sometimes known as the 'stress' hormone. Cortisol increases our blood sugar levels and raises our blood pressure, giving us a short-term energy boost that primes us to react quickly to the crisis.

When the threat has gone, another part of the autonomic nervous system, the 'parasympathetic' nervous system, calms our body back down again. It slows our heart rate, lowers blood pressure and increases blood flow back to our stomach – making it easier for us to digest food again. The parasympathetic nervous system brings us down a gear and gets our bodies back into balance.[4]

This system evolved when humans lived a hunter-gatherer existence. However, in a relatively short space of time – just a few thousand years – our lifestyles have changed dramatically – we now live in a 21st-century world of offices, cars and deadlines, rather than caves, spears and predators. While we do still face physical threats – crossing a busy road, for example – most of the pressures we experience are lower-level, chronic ones: the constant demands placed on us by our overactive world: to pay bills, or reply to emails.

These ongoing stressors don't really need the outpouring of adrenaline that running from a sabre-toothed tiger would have done, but, conditioned by millions of years of evolution, the autonomic nervous system still reacts as though we are in grave physical danger – it puts us on red alert. So, when we don't get any relief from the stress of our lives, the sympathetic nervous system stays switched on, and the parasympathetic nervous system doesn't get a chance to bring our bodies back into balance. We continue to feel stressed, and our body is constantly on overdrive. The 'fight or flight' response, which was meant to give us a short-term boost in a crisis, puts our bodies under too much pressure – with potentially serious consequences for our health. Our pulse stays too fast and our blood pressure too high, increasing our long-term risk of having a stroke or a heart attack. It dampens our immune system, making us more prone to infections, and possibly even cancer. By predisposing us to illness and putting extra strain on our bodies, long-term stress can shorten our lives. It can even damage the mechanisms that help protect and repair our DNA, speeding up the process of ageing.[5]

Meditation is one way to regulate, consciously, the autonomic nervous system and reduce the damaging effects of stress. It helps switch off our overworked sympathetic drive, relaxing blood vessels and decreasing our heart rate – reducing our risk of developing high blood pressure and cardiovascular disease. One study found that people with long-term meditation experience were up to 12 years younger than their chronological age, as measured by their blood pressure, eyesight and hearing.[6]

By deciding to take ourselves out of our usual busy mode, even for just a short while each day, we are retraining our bodies, resetting the balance between the sympathetic and parasympathetic nervous systems, and reducing the chronic stress of our 21st-century lifestyles.

A DIFFERENT KIND OF HEALTH

Conventional medicine certainly isn't ineffective. The attention to detail in the scientific process, and the care and compassion offered by health workers across the world, has brought amazing advances in the treatment of many,

many illnesses – life expectancy in the Western world over the last century has almost doubled. By drawing attention to the limitations of modern medicine, we are not trying to undermine it, nor the wonderful job done by the people who practise it, improving the quality of life for so many of us. With ever more research and improving technology, we are continually pushing the boundaries of what can be done to understand and preserve our physical health.

But even with the best doctors, the best medicine and the best technology, we still have to face the reality that we can't cure every illness. Our bodies *will* wear out, and we *will* have to face the inevitability of ageing, sickness and death. So might there be another way of relating to our health that can take better account of these realities? Might there be an approach that can help us experience a more fundamental sense of health – a genuine wholeness – even when our bodies are not in such good shape? As well as asking the mechanic to fix our body/machine, perhaps we could take a closer look at how we're driving it?

Thirty years ago, the molecular biologist Jon Kabat-Zinn began exploring some of these issues. A scientist who also practised yoga and meditation, Kabat-Zinn wondered whether mindfulness could help people who were experiencing chronic physical health problems – the people whom medicine didn't seem to help. While he knew that meditation probably wouldn't cure their pain, he felt it was worth exploring whether it might alleviate some of the stress and suffering that went with it. By teaching people how to be mindful of their bodies, could patients experience a different kind of health, even when they became ill? Could it help them not fire that second arrow of suffering on top of the first arrow of pain?

Kabat-Zinn developed a meditation programme which he later called Mindfulness-Based Stress Reduction (MBSR). Over eight weekly sessions, he taught groups of people a range of mindfulness exercises – the kind of breathing practices we explored in the last chapter, plus meditations designed to foster 'mindfulness of body'. He also taught them how to cultivate mindful awareness during activities such as eating and walking.

While most of the course participants had come to Kabat-Zinn with physical ailments, often serious or chronic long-term conditions such as heart disease, cancer, digestive problems or chronic pain – the mindfulness-based stress reduction course made no attempt to change their bodies. Many of them had come to the end of the line when it came to conventional treatment – there was nothing more that could be done to fix them from the outside. So, rather than trying to act like a specialist, focusing on a person's symptoms and trying to get rid of them, Kabat-Zinn tried a more holistic, wide-angled approach – he asked his patients to let go of trying to get better, and instead had them pay simple attention to their experience.

In his discourse on the Four Foundations of Mindfulness, the Buddha said that by practising meditation we could learn to live 'contemplating the body in the body'. By this he meant that by paying mindful attention to our body – not *thinking* about it but experiencing it – we could begin to live a more embodied existence. We could actually *be in* our bodies. Jon Kabat-Zinn was offering the same possibility to the participants in his mindfulness-based stress reduction course – by practising mindfulness, participants could stop struggling with their bodies, and learn how to really inhabit them.

Kabat-Zinn had received his own mindfulness training in a Buddhist context, but he knew that it wouldn't make sense to teach meditation to his patients as if they were Buddhists. Many wouldn't have been interested in adopting a spiritual or moral path, and others may have already had one of their own. Buddhism was still thought of by most people as a strange, foreign religion, and it certainly wouldn't have seemed appropriate to teach it in a healthcare setting.

Besides, if mindfulness really was a way of coming into greater wellbeing, then it wouldn't need any religious crutches to support it – it could stand on its own merits. Kabat-Zinn's secular approach has been endorsed by many Buddhist teachers. When he asked zen master Morinaga Roshi about the challenge of teaching mindfulness to non-Buddhists, the reply was unequivocal: 'Throw out Buddha! Throw out zen.'[7]

Even so, Mindfulness-Based Stress Reduction retained the essence of what the Buddha had taught. It was a chance to experience a kind of wholeness that is perhaps *even more* relevant now than in the Buddha's time. Living in a modern-day culture that splits off body and mind from each other, mindfulness is an alternative to the busy, problem-solving mindset that treats our bodies as something we *own* rather than something we *are*, something to fix rather than something to experience.

BEING IN OUR BODIES

By reconnecting our minds and bodies, mindfulness
is a way for us to rediscover balance. Jon Kabat-Zinn's
programme offered the chance for people to experience
the true health that comes not from trying to make our
bodies last forever, but from accepting and facing up to the
difficulties and realities of life – experiencing the present
moment fully, even when that moment might not be
pleasant. Unfortunately, we've been perpetuating the idea
of a mind–body split in our scientific and medical culture
for centuries, at least since the time of the philosopher
Descartes, who insisted that mind and body *were* separate.
Reversing such an age-old assumption is no easy feat. We
have got used to rushing around like 'heads on sticks', out
of touch with our bodies, unaware of our minds. It is an
especially difficult task when we have a chronic illness
and are under stress – exactly the time when we are most
vulnerable to our habitual patterns. In pain, desperate for
relief, sure that there must be something that can be done to
make us feel better, the temptation is to fight our bodies, or
try to escape from them – to do anything not to be *in* them.

In mindfulness meditation, contrary to all our impulses, we
let go of the attempt to be free of our pain. Instead we turn
our attention inwards, come closer to our experience, and
really see it, feel it, be with it. We actually approach the very
thing that we have been trying to get away from. We start to
feel our bodies, even when – especially when – they hurt.

Why would anyone voluntarily choose to come closer to
pain in this way? It sounds like masochism – directing our

awareness towards what is most difficult. But it can work, as an experiment carried out by Delia Cioffi and James Holloway at the University of Houston demonstrates.[8] Cioffi and Holloway wanted to examine the effects of three different ways of relating to pain – distracting awareness from it, suppressing it, and monitoring it, the last one of these being what we might call mindfulness.

First they had 63 people dip their hands in ice-cold water – then they asked some of their subjects to think about their bedroom at home (distraction), some to try to stop themselves from thinking about the pain in their hands (suppression), and the rest simply to pay close attention to the sensations they were experiencing (monitoring). Cioffi and Holloway found that the group who were asked to be mindful and monitor the sensations in their hands recovered fastest, and those who tried to suppress the pain recovered most slowly.

And that was not all – the pain-suppressors had a lower threshold for interpreting a simple vibration as painful when exposed to it later on. So trying not to think about pain seems to *heighten* our experience of it rather than lessening it, and actually makes us more sensitive to it in the long run.

When we struggle with bodily pain, either by trying to fight it or suppress it, that pain can become all-consuming – we are heaping suffering on top of it, until it feels like all we are is pain. But by watching pain, accepting it, being mindful of it, we are creating a different kind of space in which to experience it – one that is less stressful and more open.

Held in the space of this mindful environment, the pain in our body looms less large – unpleasant, perhaps, but only a part of our experience.

BODY MINDFULNESS

Let's try some body mindfulness now. First, settle with a few moments of mindfulness of breathing. Take a strong, relaxed and comfortable posture – wherever you happen to be reading this book – and begin paying attention to your breath. Feel each in-breath as it enters your body, and each out-breath as you exhale, just as we have already practised. Let go of thinking – all the ideas, judgements, plans and memories that are running through your mindstream. Just notice thoughts as they pass through, resting your attention gently on the breath.

Now, as you continue to breathe mindfully, see if you can pay attention to any sensations in your body. If you're sitting or lying on something, how does the contact with your skin feel? Going deeper than your skin, how do the insides of your body feel, right at this moment? Perhaps there's a sense of relaxation and calm in some places, or maybe tension, tightness, or holding on somewhere? Perhaps there's a part of your body that's in pain? If so, what kind of pain is it – is it a long, dull ache or a repeating, sharp kind of pain? See if you can investigate the texture of the sensations without getting caught up in thoughts about what it means, or whether you like it or dislike it. Does it change at all while you are paying mindful attention to it – is it solid, or is it subtly moving, ebbing and flowing? Or maybe you don't feel any sensations in your body at all – if so, then just notice *that*.

However your body feels, just be aware of it, be with it, be it. Stay with that experience, just for a minute or two.

What is your body telling you? Does it feel relaxed or under pressure? If it feels tense, were you aware of that tension before you began paying attention in this way? Are there any feelings of pain or discomfort – if there are, what messages might that be giving you about what you need to do to look after yourself?

Now, take your awareness to one specific area of the body. If you like, it can be somewhere you noticed there was some tension or pain. Or, if that feels difficult, or you don't feel any tension or pain in your body at the moment, take your awareness to a part of the body where you feel relaxed and calm, or where you don't feel any particular sensations. Whichever region you choose, gently direct your mind's attention to it. Be really curious about that part of the body. If it's your right arm, notice the sensations in your elbow, your forearm, your shoulder. What's it really like to have a right arm at the moment – how does it feel when you bring your mind's eye to it? If you choose your neck, your right leg, your stomach or your chest, then just notice the sensations in *that* area of the body.

Stay with your experience for a few minutes, maintaining your attention on the area you have chosen, carefully, gently and with interest. See if you can lean into your experience a little – move your mind towards it, approach it, be close to it. If you find yourself having any thoughts or judgements about what you are doing, let those just be there as they pass through your mind, as we have been letting any other thoughts pass through our minds in the mindfulness of breathing practice – without getting caught up in them.

How did it feel, first to pay attention to the whole of the body, and then to this one particular area? Perhaps it's an area that you usually ignore, that you sometimes forget is really part of you? Or perhaps it's an area that you're always focusing on, getting angry with, or trying to fix and make better? What was it like just to hold it in awareness for a while, experiencing it and letting it be as it is? Scary? Boring? Frustrating? Annoying? Enjoyable? How was it to notice those feelings without buying into any stories you might create around them – to stay in the experience without intellectualising it?

This kind of mindfulness of body technique is useful not just when we are in pain, but whenever we have any kind of stress in our bodies. And isn't that most of us, most of the time? How many of us experience tension – in our jaws, shoulders, legs or neck – but get so used to it that we aren't even aware that it's there.

When we are mindful of our body, it is a bit like taking its temperature, listening to what it has to tell us. Physical symptoms are often useful feedback messages that let us know we are under stress and need to change some aspect of how we are living. If we are out of touch with our bodies, we are less likely to take notice of those messages, and they may start to become more insistent in their attempt to get our mind's attention! By reconnecting with our bodies in mindfulness, we don't need to wait until they break down before we start hearing what they need. By practising mindfulness of body, we might start to realise when we need to rest, when we need to eat more healthily or when we need to exercise – not based on what we are told is good for us, but by listening to our bodies ourselves.

PRACTICE: Connecting Mind and Body

In the Four Foundations of Mindfulness, the Buddha taught that health could be cultivated by the simple practice of connecting mind and body. Versions of this exercise, sometimes known as a body scan, have long been practised by Buddhists, and are also now practised in MBSR and other secular mindfulness-based courses. By helping develop mindful awareness of each physical part of us in turn, it's a way of making and deepening the mind–body connection. It's best not to rush this practice – usually it's recommended to take between 25 and 45 minutes for the whole exercise, from start to finish. It can also help to be guided through this and other mindfulness practices, especially when you first start meditating. We've created audio instructions for many of the practices in this book – they are available from our website at www.themindfulmanifesto.com.

STEP ONE

Find a place where you can lie down comfortably, perhaps on a soft carpet on the floor or, if the weather is warm and you can find a quiet place, on a rug outside. Lying in or on a bed is also fine. Cover yourself with a blanket if it helps you keep warm. Close your eyes gently, and begin by practising mindfulness of breathing for a minute or so, allowing your body to let go into the surface you are lying on – feel your body being supported from beneath, noticing the body's contact with the floor, bed or rug.

STEP TWO
As you breathe, bring a gentle attention to your whole body. Experience any sensations you might be having in the body, allowing them to be as they are. Especially notice how the sensations of breathing feel, as we practised in the last chapter. Allow your mind and body to be one with your breathing.

STEP THREE
Now see if you can direct your awareness gently down your left leg, into your left foot and towards your left big toe. If it helps, you could cultivate the sense that you are now breathing down into your toe, and as you move your awareness round the body, that you are taking your breath with you, as you breathe into each part of the body in turn. With your mind resting in your toe for now, notice any sensations you might be feeling there. Stay with that for a minute or two. If your mind wanders away from awareness of the left big toe, just notice that and gently bring it back, in the same way that you would bring your awareness back to the breath when you are practising mindfulness of breathing.

STEP FOUR
As you take an in-breath, gradually expand your awareness into each other area of the left foot in turn, and then to the whole of the left foot. If you have any thoughts about your experience, whether they are negative or positive, just notice those, too.

STEP FIVE

Now, bringing your awareness up to the left ankle, notice any sensations you might be experiencing in this area. Once again, if your mind wanders away from awareness of this part of the body, just notice that and bring your mind back – remember, mind-wandering isn't wrong or bad – if your mind didn't wander, you wouldn't have the chance to practise returning to mindfulness! Now, gradually, holding your awareness for a while on each part of the body in turn, move your awareness gently up through the left leg, up the left shin and calf, to the left knee, and then to the left thigh. If you find there are any particular sensations in any of part of the body – tingling, itching, tension, pain or pleasant sensations – just be curious about those.

Repeat steps three to five with the right toe, right foot and right leg.

STEP SIX

Having reconnected with your legs in this way, move your awareness up through the pelvic area, to the genitals, buttocks and hips. Notice any resistance you might have to bringing your awareness to these areas. Now, move your awareness to your stomach, an area where many of us feel our emotions strongly. How does your gut feel right now – is it full, empty or somewhere in between? Is there any sensation of calm or disturbance? Do you notice how your breathing is being experienced in your stomach – deeper or more shallow?

STEP SEVEN

Now, connecting once again with your breathing, move your awareness further up the front of the body, staying with the sensations in each region for a while. Bring your mind's eye to the chest, to the throat, to the neck and to the face, in turn, perhaps noticing any tension in these areas and being with the breath as it passes through, in and out. Can you feel both the inside and outside of your body – the muscles, organs, bones and skin that make up these areas? From your face, move your awareness up to the top of your head, your skull, and then down the back of your head, to the top of your spine. How is it to pay attention to your head in this way – not thinking about the head, but just experiencing how it is, this amazing part of the body that holds and processes so much of our mental activity?

STEP EIGHT

From the head, take your awareness now to the shoulders, an area where many of us hold tension, and notice how the muscles feel there. From your shoulders, take your awareness to your arms, each in turn, down each forearm, into each elbow, to each wrist, to each hand, then to each one of the fingers in each hand, just as you did with your toes earlier. Then, once you have rested your awareness for a while in both of the hands, move your mindful attention to the back, and gradually down the spine that holds your upper body together. How do the muscles in your back feel as you take your awareness to this area?

STEP NINE

Finally, expand your mind out gradually from the small of your back to the whole of your body. If you like, you could synchronise the expansion of your awareness with a series of out-breaths, slowly taking your attention wider and wider until you are holding the whole of your body in awareness. Notice how it feels to bring your attention out, once again beginning to experience the whole of your body and mind together, not separate but integrated. Stay with that for a while, perhaps imagining that your body and mind are breathing together, in awareness, in harmony.

STEP TEN
When you are ready, slowly open your eyes to the world. Perhaps first taking a look around at your environment, being mindful of what you find there, gently roll over onto your side, and then, begin to lift up your body and sit up. Take a few moments to reconnect to the wider world as you come out of the practice.

Each time you practise mindfulness of body like this, see if you can maintain some awareness of the interrelationship between your body and mind as you go about the rest of your day. Whatever you are doing, explore the sense that these aspects of your being are not separate. This is actually how the Buddha instructed his students to practise, to be mindful of their bodies not just when they were formally meditating – sitting or lying down – but when they were going about their daily business.

In the stress-reduction clinic, Jon Kabat-Zinn and his colleagues gave their patients a new kind of power to work *with* rather than against their bodies – whatever very real difficulties these people were facing. Whether they were living with chronic pain, fatigue, heart disease or cancer, they could reduce their stress and suffering by coming into awareness of their situation fully and gently. Their illnesses might present them with great challenges, but by seeing with a fresh perspective of mindfulness, they could respond differently, and reduce their suffering.

The clinic was a huge success – patients who had previously felt defeated often reported new hope, perhaps not a cure but a way of living more peacefully with their condition. Their progress was often amazing – after years of feeling disabled by illness, many patients began to accept their bodies, carving out new and fulfilling lives as they worked within the limitations set by their situation, rather than fighting it or trying to ignore it.

The stories were heartening, but to have a chance of being accepted in medical circles, the mindfulness-based stress reduction programme had to stand up to scientific scrutiny – it needed to be tested empirically. And because it had a simple, clear and easily replicable course format, it lent itself more easily to clinical research. Whereas the results of previous studies on 'meditation' were often obscured by confusion as to what exactly was being studied, the MBSR course format was straightforward and well-structured. Many patients could be put through exactly the same training, and by evaluating how they responded, it was possible to study whether mindfulness really was helping people.

Study after study has now shown that MBSR does indeed reduce stress and help people deal with their symptoms.[9] In one US inner-city trial (in Meriden, Connecticut), participants' anxiety levels fell by 70 per cent after they took the course.[10] Not only that, but their reported medical symptoms reduced by 44 per cent – they also visited their doctor much less often after their mindfulness training. The effects seem to be long-lasting, too – another trial found that not only did participants get less anxious during and after the course, but they were still feeling the benefits three years later.[11]

The MBSR programme also helps people enjoy a more harmonious relationship with their bodies.[12] In one of Kabat-Zinn's studies, participants were asked to rate how far they considered each part of their body to be problematic. At the end of the course, the scores had fallen by around 30 per cent, suggesting that these patients' minds and bodies were no longer in such a state of struggle.

JULIE'S EXPERIENCE

Julie is 35 and has a serious inflammatory condition of the bowel called Crohn's disease, which she has suffered from since she was a teenager. There is no cure, and, when it flares up, it causes a lot of pain. Julie relapsed five years ago and has been unwell ever since.

Stress makes Julie's condition worse. 'With Crohn's disease you feel physically really unwell. I was working in a very tough job and I would drink Diet Coke or coffee to get through the day. I would come home and just collapse. In the end my health totally crashed and I was unable to continue working.'

Julie referred herself to a mindfulness course at King's College Hospital, London. She says that the meditation practices have helped her see the effect her thinking and lifestyle were having on her body. 'I clearly saw my thinking patterns for the first time and how they increased my anxiety and negative feelings about my illness. I was using my job as a way of avoiding having to deal with anxiety. I think that's the thing about meditation, combined with CBT – it very gently helps you question some of your thinking. Mindfulness was able to help me separate my thinking from reality; I now make very different, more gentle choices about how I care for myself and spend my time. I will never return to such a stressful environment.'

Mindfulness has also helped Julie learn to listen to her body a lot more. 'I had denied my Crohn's disease for a long time. Mindfulness practice has allowed me to accept my condition and recognise that I am physically quite ill. Ignoring what my body was trying to tell me was just damaging me further.'

From being in a place where her mind and body were not very connected, Julie now feels much more at peace with herself. 'I have gone from seeing it as this thing that I didn't want to deal with – an inconvenience – to it now being part of me. It's a much more accepting relationship. Rather than seeing it as a kind of hindrance –

something to get annoyed with myself at – I can be more compassionate to myself, my body, and my situation.

'It has changed my life in such a positive way. My meditation practice has become an integral part of my day, my anxiety levels continue to lessen, and it has had an impact on my health, which I now try to deal with a day at a time.'

HOW DOES IT WORK?

So, people report less stress once they have learned how to practise mindfulness. But what is actually going on in their bodies? In the last chapter, we showed how neuroscience is suggesting that being mindful seems to have a measurable impact on the brain. Can the signs of reduced stress that have been reported over and over again also be demonstrated by the material evidence of people's bodies?

Some of the first research to investigate this was carried out by Jon Kabat-Zinn together with a team of dermatologists. They studied a group of patients with psoriasis – a common skin condition which produces 'plaques' of thickened, red scaly skin on the body.[13] The cause of psoriasis still isn't clear, but it is known to be made worse by stress. It also seems likely that the body's immune system plays an important part in the development of the condition. The immune system is normally responsible for protecting us from harm, but in patients with psoriasis, cells from the immune system build up in the skin, releasing chemicals that cause inflammation and an overgrowth of skin cells in the affected area.

Most treatments for psoriasis try to reduce the inflammation or dampen the immune system by slowing down the growth of skin cells. This is usually done with creams that are applied to the plaques, but if the psoriasis is widespread, patients may be given ultraviolet-light treatment called *phototherapy*. Given that stress usually makes psoriasis worse, Jon Kabat-Zinn and his colleagues wanted to find out if practising mindfulness could have the opposite effect, and enhance the effect of phototherapy.

The researchers divided the patients into two groups, and while one set received their usual light treatment, the others were also guided through a set of mindfulness meditation techniques – played on a tape as the patients stood in the phototherapy booth. Pictures were taken of the psoriasis before the treatment started, and again at regular intervals throughout the trial, until the plaques had disappeared.

The results were striking: the skin of the patients who practised mindfulness while receiving phototherapy cleared up to four times more quickly than those who had the light treatment alone.

More evidence that mindfulness can affect the immune system came from one of the studies we looked at in the last chapter. Remember the employees at Promega in Wisconsin, from whom Richard Davidson took EEG brain readings before and after they had trained in mindfulness? At the same time Davidson was examining the workers' brains, Kabat-Zinn was injecting them with a flu vaccination.

Vaccinations work by stimulating the immune system to produce antibodies to a virus, which are then able to recognise and destroy that same virus if it gets into the body again. The stronger the immune system a person has, the greater the antibody response produced to the vaccination. Previous studies had shown that being under stress could lower the antibody response, and Kabat-Zinn's team wanted to see if mindfulness could increase it.

The scientists gave vaccinations to each of the Promega participants at the end of their mindfulness-based stress reduction course, as well as to some of their colleagues who hadn't received the training. A few weeks later, the flu antibody level in their bloodstream was tested. The group who had learned how to be mindful had a higher response than those who had not taken part in the course. Not only that, but the same participants whose brain activity had shown the greatest change from right to left (indicating a shift towards greater wellbeing) were also those who produced the strongest response to the flu jab.

If practising mindfulness can help our immune system handle illnesses like psoriasis and the flu, can it also help us cope with more serious conditions, like cancer or HIV? It seems so. Linda Witek-Janusek and her colleagues in Chicago offered an MBSR course to 38 women after they'd had surgery for breast cancer, and then compared their recovery to that of another 31 women.[14] Witek-Janusek found that the women who took the MBSR course had lower levels of the stress hormone cortisol, and that their immune systems recovered more quickly after their treatment – they showed a higher level of what is called 'natural killer cell activity'. Natural killer cells can recognise and destroy cancer cells – the more active they are, the better the chance of being able to completely clear the cancer, and prevent it from returning.

And at the University of California, David Creswell examined the effects of mindfulness meditation on the immune systems of 48 people with HIV.[15] They measured the patients' levels of CD4 T cells, which help coordinate the immune system when it has to respond to a threat. These are the cells that the HIV virus destroys, damaging the immune system and leaving people prone to infections and cancers that could otherwise be easily fought off. Creswell found that the levels of CD4 T cells in participants who had eight weeks of mindfulness training remained constant during the course, compared to a control group whose CD4 T cell count dropped. He also found that those participants who did the most mindfulness practice during the period of the course showed the greatest benefit to their immune systems.

HELPING WITH PAIN

Mindfulness certainly isn't a cure for cancer or HIV, but there is evidence that practising mindfulness can help boost our body's ability to heal itself. But what about pain? Most of the people who came to Jon Kabat-Zinn's clinic were reporting some kind of physical pain, which conventional medicine had not been able to alleviate. Even though MBSR made no attempt to remove participants' pain, by learning a different way of relating to it – experiencing it without judgement, without getting angry at it or trying to get rid of it – might the participants come to interpret their pain in a different way, and be less troubled by it? It would seem so. Compared to control groups, clinical pain patients have reported feeling less pain at the end of an MBSR course, as well as being less restricted by their pain. Research at the stress reduction clinic found that 65 per cent of patients who hadn't responded to standard medical treatments were less troubled by pain after learning mindfulness.[16]

Jon Kabat-Zinn's approach has been revolutionary. While people have been reporting for thousands of years that meditation practices enable them to feel less stressed and more physically healthy, such claims would never have been admissible as scientific evidence. These reports might have provided an interesting anecdote or case study, and even encouraged some people to take up the practice for themselves, but until they were empirically tested, they were never going to be enough to convince the mainstream medical system that it was worth teaching to patients. Unless it was possible to present the benefits of mindfulness in these terms, it would never shake off its image as an otherworldly, 'spiritual' practice, even though mindfulness is actually about relating with the here and now.

But Jon Kabat-Zinn is both a scientist and a meditator. He knew that while the rich inner experience of practising mindfulness might never be fully captured by material evidence, its benefits could be shown scientifically. He took the essence of what the Buddha had taught about mindfulness, stripped it of any associations that might be deemed religious, and presented it in a format that would enable it to sit comfortably within the healthcare system. He then collected the data that shows, on medicine's own terms, that mindfulness works. In doing so, he opened up the benefits of mindfulness to a vast number of people who would probably never otherwise have practised it. More than 17,000 people have taken the stress reduction course at what is now the Centre for Mindfulness in Medicine, Health Care and Society at the University of Massachusetts Medical School.

A FRUITFUL DIALOGUE

By putting mindfulness under the microscope, Kabat-Zinn has made it possible for medicine and meditation to engage in fruitful dialogue. Scientific data may not reflect the deep learning which comes from those 'Aha' moments when new practitioners realise that they can begin to relax with their bodies, even when they are in pain – but increasingly it can and does provide objective evidence for what people describe: a reduction in stress and medical symptoms, and an increase in their ability to manage and enjoy their bodily health – and that is the gold standard by which our culture judges the worth of a healthcare treatment.

Mindfulness-based stress reduction represents the possibility of a paradigm shift in how we approach our health. Not only does it help us bring together body and mind, but it also encourages the integration of two great traditions that can help us experience wellbeing: the amazing advances of medical science, representing the great possibilities of activity, improvement and the scientific method, and the profound realisations of mindfulness practice, representing the wisdom of contemplation, acceptance and seeing beyond temporary material circumstances to a deep wholeness that is not dependent on bodily health. With the combination of these two approaches – a kind of contemplative medicine – we can begin to learn how to manifest, how to truly *be*, even when we are experiencing pain. And if we can do that, we will dramatically reduce our stress and our suffering.

MINDFULNESS TRAINING AND THE NHS

Offering mindfulness training for physical health problems has so far been a predominantly American phenomenon – MBSR is now being taught in hundreds of hospitals across the United States. But it could also make a big difference to the UK healthcare system, which is overwhelmed by chronic stress-related illness. It has been estimated that 'medically unexplained' illnesses alone cost the NHS around £8 billion a year.[17] People who suffer from these conditions go to their GPs far more often than most, and are twice as likely to attend hospital outpatient clinics and Accident and Emergency departments.[18]

Poorly served by a system that tries and fails to diagnose and treat them according to conventional methods, these people incur huge costs, both to themselves, in terms of their own suffering, and to society, through spinning round and round a system that doesn't know what to do with them. Mindfulness training will not cure them – it doesn't claim to – but it might help reduce their stress levels and help them better come to terms with their pain.

Good medical care means encouraging people to look after their own health – if we are to lighten the load on our overstretched health service, we need to take responsibility for our own wellbeing as much as possible. When we treat our bodies just as machines to be taken to the garage for servicing and repairs, we are disempowering ourselves – handing over the keys to our health to somebody else. That is bad news for us, it is bad news for doctors, and it is bad news for our health services. Of course, we should use the technologies of conventional medicine to fix people's bodies when we can, but, by teaching powerful mind-training techniques that help us create good health from the inside, we could move towards an optimum usage of both 'doing' and 'being' approaches to healthcare, helping bring our medical system, and our bodies, into balance.

Most of us know instinctively that this mind–body approach to healthcare suits us – we know the effect that stress has on our bodies, and we can feel the strain lift when we let go of it. Perhaps this is why mindfulness is such a popular approach with patients – despite making considerable demands on them (up to 45 minutes 'homework' a day), an average of around 85 per cent of MBSR course participants complete the course, and around three-quarters of people are still practising some of the meditations up to four years later.[19]

If training in mindfulness-based stress reduction were offered to everyone who experiences chronic bodily illness, medically explained or not, the rewards could be enormous. It could help people cope more effectively with the often huge pressures of managing their pain. It could give their bodies the best chance of recovery, boosting their immune systems and reducing the long-term damage caused by stress. It could save some of the enormous resources that are currently spent on dealing, often ineffectively, with stress-related illnesses, and enable us to redirect those resources more appropriately. Perhaps most importantly, practising mindfulness of body could help all of us cultivate a deeper appreciation of the amazing experience of actually *having* a physical body, as well as a mind that can experience it.

MINDFULNESS OF BODY: SUGGESTIONS FOR PRACTICE

TAKING YOUR TIME
The human body is one of the most intricate, complex and fascinating creations in the known universe, and you have it with you all day, every day. By paying mindful attention to it, you have an opportunity to really experience *being* such an amazing creation – why not take the time to appreciate that? If you can, set aside 20 minutes or more for mindfulness of body practice, creating space to really connect with each part of your body.

FALLING AWAKE
If you have a tendency to fall asleep during this exercise, try practising with your eyes open. If you are in bed, perhaps move to another location less associated with sleep. The practice can also be done sitting up or even standing. Don't give yourself a hard time for falling asleep – perhaps that's what your body is saying you need!

NOT 'TRYING' TO RELAX
If you are relaxed when you practise, that's fine. If not, that's just the way it is. However you feel, your only job is to

notice and be aware of the sensations in your body. As an instructor once told us: 'Just practise the technique. What happens next is none of your business!'

CULTIVATING THE ART OF BODY ACCEPTANCE

In mindfulness meditation, we let go of 'judging' our bodies. When we treat ourselves as machines, we tend to see illness as a malfunction – a *bad* thing. In mindfulness meditation, we don't judge what comes up in our experience as 'good' or 'bad', we just notice it, experiencing whatever is happening without making evaluations of it. If you feel angry at your body for being in pain, fear at the idea of investigating your body more closely, or irritation at the practice itself – or even if you feel chilled out and 'at one' with your body – just notice these experiences, without adding a mental storyline to them.

STAYING WITH DISCOMFORT

If you experience pain or uncomfortable sensations, see whether you can resist the first temptation to give up, shift position or take a break – see if it is possible to hold the discomfort in your awareness. At the same time, meditation is not meant to be a torture session – if you find yourself gritting your teeth or tempted to risk injury to carry on, then your practice has become too tight. Give yourself a break.

LETTING GO OF RESULTS ...

If the body hurts during practice, that isn't a 'bad' meditation, just as having a pleasant body experience doesn't make it a 'good' meditation. By letting go of the ideas of success or failure, we are letting go of the 'doing' mind that judges our experience by results.

... AND MAINTAINING MOTIVATION

The realisation that mindfulness isn't a quick fix can be a disappointment, especially if we are hoping it will cure our pain. Mindfulness is major work – its rewards take time to emerge. Don't give up if your practice doesn't instantly make you feel better – it's another opportunity to let go of being attached to results, and to simply be with whatever is.

Jonty's Experience

Mindfulness of body is not just about treating illness or managing physical symptoms. Increasing our awareness of our bodies, as with our breath, helps anchor us in the present moment. I've found that it's a particularly good practice during exercise. I've always tried to keep physically active, but living in London and not really having a 'runner's physique' means that I tend to rely on going to the gym to keep fit. My usual approach is to spend some time on the treadmill, trying to distract myself from all the unpleasant sensations I am feeling in my body by listening to music or watching the TV screen above me. Then I go and pull and push, lift and squeeze my muscles on various machines whilst I daydream about the six-pack I want. It's a pretty mindless process. While the simple act of raising my pulse rate will still be benefiting my heart, this approach to exercise doesn't really engage my body and my mind – if anything, it further disconnects me from my body – I treat it like a machine, and in the long term I risk injury and damage rather than health and fitness.

With the help of Julien, a personal trainer, I have recently started to discover that, as a result of not paying

attention to my body over time, I have been overusing
a lot of the 'wrong' muscles. Years of rowing at school
mean that I have been using my shoulders and my legs
disproportionately, and still do whenever I exercise. Even
during sit-ups I try and work with my shoulders and my
legs, not my stomach! As I have become more mindful
of my body I have tried to identify the muscles I use and
move my effort more to my core, gradually loosening my
shoulders and hips and using my body in a much more
efficient way. I am also now able to identify the 'good
pain' of muscles stretching or working, from the 'bad
pain' of tension in the wrong places risking damage.
Julien has helped me to vary what I do, avoid repetitive
movements and engage my mind and my body in the
process. And, of course, the advantage of exercising
mindfully is that it also helps me stay in the present
moment, not only reducing the risk of injuring myself but
also resting my mind from worries about work or what
needs doing at home. In this way exercise becomes
something I do to take care of myself rather than a
punishment for having had an extra chocolate biscuit!
So, although I may not have that six-pack I always
wanted, I do feel healthier and happier.

Ed's Experience

Like Jonty, I am lucky enough to connect with my body
through sport and exercise. I've always loved playing
football, tennis, squash – or going running or swimming.
I believe part of the reason I found physical exercise
so enjoyable when I was growing up was that it was
about the only time that I allowed my body and mind
to synchronise – as any sportsperson will tell you, it's

difficult to play well if your mind is elsewhere. The best players are right 'in the zone' – fully in flow with the direct experience of their minds, bodies and the game.

But it was only when I started meditating that I really began to pay attention to my body in a mindful way. At first, it was uncomfortable – there was tension in my shoulders and jaw that had probably always been there, but which I had never been aware of. It was hard to sit there and accept that my body was not as calm as I'd thought. But it also made sense of many of the symptoms of stress that I had manifested over the years – I could see how bodily tension had led to my frequent migraines, for example. I also realised how my bouts of depression were far more than a mental phenomenon – my whole body protested when I took on too much. By becoming aware of my body, I gained access to an internal warning system that tells me when I need to slow down or take a break. I admit I don't always listen to it – the compulsion to cram 40 hours' activity into a 24-hour day is still compelling – but at least I have a chance: before mindfulness, I didn't even hear what my body was saying. My body is no longer just a machine to flog to death.

CHAPTER FOUR

MINDFULNESS OF MIND

Notice and nurture your mind – by being mindful of your mind, you can train in living more happily, and help protect yourself from problems like depression and anxiety.

To live a happy life, we need to keep our minds in good shape. Just as taking exercise and eating a balanced diet can help our bodies stay well, so there are simple steps we can take to foster a healthy mind. Unfortunately, because most of us focus much less on our mental health than we do on our physical condition, we often end up unconsciously perpetuating patterns of mind that lead to unhappiness. We've already seen how this can be bad for us physically; for our minds, the consequences can be just as bad, if not worse.

Mental health problems are one of the unacknowledged scourges of our time – in the UK, one in five of us is likely to suffer with depression at some point in our lives.[1] The problem is a global one: according to the World Health Organisation, around 450 million people around the planet have a diagnosable mental health problem, and by the year 2030, depression will have become the world's biggest cause of disability.[2] Mental illness as a whole is thought to cost the British economy around £100 billion a year.[3]

These kinds of figures can't really convey the suffering of people who experience depression, anxiety or other unhappy mind states, or the stress it causes those around them. As well as being an awful experience in itself, poor mental health can lead to broken relationships, damaged careers, despair, self-harm and, in extreme cases, suicide. On a subtler level it can spark reckless behaviour, unnecessary arguments and mistakes through poor concentration or lack of care. Whichever way you look at it, mental illness means misery.

Like many of the physical health issues discussed in the last chapter, mental illness tends not to get 'cured'. The more a person gets depressed, the more likely a recurrence becomes – around half the people who get depressed once will have another episode at some point in their lives, and someone who has been depressed three or more times faces a nine out of ten chance of becoming ill again. A full quarter of people who are depressed now will still be depressed in two years' time.[4]

There is evidence that the phenomenon of neuroplasticity is working both ways here: just as some positive experiences change the brain in ways that make us happier and healthier, negative experiences can alter the brain in ways that are less welcome. In people who have a history of severe depression, for example, structural differences (such as smaller hippocampi) have been observed even after the depression has resolved.[5] Some of the brain differences observed in people prone to depression are also associated with the length of time the person has been unwell – suggesting some causal link.

Whatever the mechanisms behind it, there is no doubt that mental health problems tend to be either recurring or chronic. It isn't easy for us to fix our minds.

AN UNHAPPINESS EPIDEMIC

Official mental health statistics are just the tip of the iceberg – how many more of us may not meet the clinical criteria for a diagnosis of depression or anxiety, but would equally be unable to class ourselves as truly 'happy'? Very few people are deeply content – most of us remain unfulfilled, insecure or troubled by a sense of inadequacy, or we feel stressed, argumentative and critical. We tend to focus on our regrets, and worry that we are missing out on opportunities that will turn into regrets at some point in the future. Many of us now compare our lives, not just to those of our neighbours, but to people we have never met – celebrities who seem to epitomise our fantasies of how we would like to be. And so our own achievements, rather than being delighted in, are met with only brief satisfaction and leave us longing for more.

Some of us aren't even prepared to *talk* about our mental health – whereas the cast on a broken leg might be proudly displayed for friends to sign, problems like depression get hidden away – when we admit to a mental illness, we risk people thinking us weak, stupid or self-indulgent. Perhaps we have made some progress from the days when people with mental health problems were basically discarded, locked up in asylums where no one could see them, but the reluctance to take looking after our minds seriously is there for anyone to measure – just 12 per cent of NHS resources are spent on mental health services.[6] That means we spend barely a tenth of the amount on looking after our minds that we do on our bodies! No wonder we are in the midst of an unhappiness epidemic!

If we want to live a saner life, we need to break the mental health taboo. We need to be willing to really investigate our minds, to understand what creates wellbeing, and take steps to bring those conditions about in our lives, as best we can.

FACTORS INFLUENCING MENTAL HEALTH

There are many different factors that influence our mental health, some of which we have more control over than others. We are affected by our common genetic inheritance – our ancestors have passed down evolutionary strategies that have been developed and reinforced over thousands of years. Unfortunately, these habitual patterns are often so strongly ingrained that we continue to revert to them even when they aren't helpful any more. We saw this with the 'fight or flight' stress response described in the last chapter

– when the main pressures we encounter are insidious and ongoing rather than sudden and short-lived, this automatic body response can lead to chronic stress rather than a short-term boost in alertness.

We also learn from those around us as we grow up – we're much more likely to suffer from mental health problems if our parents have as well. This is partly due to the genes they passed on to us, but also because the people around when we are young act as role models – we receive our first and most important mental training lessons from them. We copy the styles of our parents – and if they respond to difficulties in their lives with depression, anxiety or anger, we are more likely to do the same.

We then receive further conditioning from our schools, from our peer group of friends, and from the media – whatever the environment we experience when growing up, it rubs off on us. We create our own self-image based on how the elders we respect and love respond to us – if we feel unloved or ignored, we may see ourselves as inadequate; if we are beaten or otherwise abused, we might internalise the idea that we are 'bad'. We develop a sense of ourselves based on how we are treated.

The effect of our surroundings on mental health continues throughout life. While some of us have minds that are more prone to unhappiness, most of us can be tipped over the edge if we face enough pressure. If we lose our job, our relationship breaks up, our body becomes sick or a loved friend or relative dies, it puts a strain on our minds.

According to the New Economics Foundation – a UK-based think-tank that works to research and improve the nation's wellbeing – around 60 per cent of our mental wellbeing comes from this combination of our genetic inheritance, upbringing, and life circumstances.[7]

This may seem like bad news: our minds are strongly influenced by factors we can't really control. However, the good news is that the other 40 per cent is influenced by our 'outlook and activities'. In other words, by the way in which we respond to our situation. If we are able to nurture attitudes and activities that create happiness, then we are much more likely to become happy. It's a bit like playing poker – there is some luck involved, but also plenty of skill in how we choose to play the cards we are dealt. With practice, by *training* our minds, we can become more skilful at how we play our hand.

THE HABIT OF HAPPINESS

Increasingly, we have scientific evidence about what promotes happiness. Whereas psychologists used to concentrate mainly on studying what made people mentally ill, some researchers have started studying mental wellbeing from the other angle – looking at what makes us *contented*. And what they have discovered is that the kinds of 'outlooks and activities' that help us enjoy healthier minds are exactly those that have been advocated by great teachers and philosophers for thousands of years.

Based on research from this new science of 'positive psychology', the UK government has created a five-a-day checklist of simple steps that people can take to look after their mental health – a diet for mental wellbeing, just as we have a five-a-day recommended diet of fruit and vegetables.[8] To be more mentally healthy, according to this list, the most important things we can all do are:

1. Connect

2. Keep Learning

3. Exercise

4. Give

5. Notice.

In other words, we can become happier by developing good friendships, by continuing to learn new things, by looking after our bodies, by being kind to others, and by being *mindful*.

Yes, being mindful. The recommendation to 'notice' in the mental health diet is actually a call to practise mindfulness. Here is what the New Economics Foundation, who helped the Government devise this five-a-day plan, say about how to 'notice':

'Be curious. Catch sight of the beautiful. Remark on the unusual. Notice the changing seasons. Savour the moment, whether you are walking to work, eating lunch or talking to friends. Be aware of the world around you and what you are feeling. Reflecting on your experiences will help you appreciate what matters to you.

'Research has shown that practising awareness of sensations, thoughts and feelings can improve both the knowledge we have about ourselves and our wellbeing for several years. But the twenty-first century's never-ending flow of messages from companies advertising products and services leaves little opportunity to savour or reflect on our experiences.'[9]

Sounds familiar, doesn't it? The New Economics Foundation are saying that by noticing more, being mindful, we can become more aware of what makes us well. With mindfulness, we will be more able to resist the pressure to be speedy that our busy society and our habitual patterns have created. We will be less likely to crave things that we can't get and don't need, and we will find greater contentment and happiness through living in the present rather than the past or the future.

Mindfulness is actually the key to all of the other parts of this mental health prescription – after all, unless we pay attention to our minds, we are unlikely to be able to slow down long enough to start behaving differently. Even if we want to build stronger relationships, exercise more, keep learning or be kinder to others, we'll find it tough. We can see how this happens with even the simplest piece of advice on the list – exercise, which has been shown to be good for both our minds and our bodies. How many of us have resolved that we'll start going to the gym, take up a new sport or cycle to work, only for our resolve to last a matter of months, weeks or even days? Despite our best intentions, we keep reverting to what we've always done, helplessly repeating the same patterns of behaviour over and over again. Mindfulness is not going to get us to the gym – only we can do that – but it can allow us to notice what we are avoiding, and why, in a less critical way.

Practising mindfulness is a courageous step towards countering the force of psychological momentum from our genetics, our upbringing and all the pressures of our over-active world. Mindfulness provides a means to actually investigate our minds, to watch how they create wellbeing and how they drive us to activities that are not good for us. At the same time, by teaching us how to direct our attention consciously, mindfulness tones up our mental muscles, giving us greater strength and flexibility to choose what we want to focus on, rather than being in thrall to what we usually do.

OBSERVING OUR THOUGHTS AND OUR MIND

When the Buddha recommended that his students practise mindfulness of mind, he was showing them that it was possible to become aware of our minds in the same way as we can become aware of our bodies. In mindfulness, we learn how to watch the contents of our mind *with our mind*. When we do this, we gradually become more aware that there is a part of our consciousness that is *not caught up* with the seemingly endless stream of thoughts that usually preoccupies us. We discover that, just as there is more to us than our bodies, there is more to us than our thoughts.

This process of watching the mind is sometimes described as 'turning the eyeballs inwards'. By practising watching our thoughts, we are using our minds in a different way – not attaching to or judging our mental experience, nor treating it as the sum total of who we are. We start to see that thoughts are not 'facts' but just one more ever-changing part of our whole being. By allowing ourselves the space to observe our thoughts, we can choose whether to believe or follow them, or to let them go. This gives us more power over our lives.

Perhaps you've found this already as you've been practising mindfulness of your breathing or body. Maybe you've seen that, while thoughts are running through your mind, it is still possible to place some of your attention on the movement of the in-and-out breath, or on a part of your body. In mindfulness meditation, we see that our thoughts are not solid – they arise, hang around for a while, and dissolve – and that there is another part of our mind that can watch it all happening. When people start meditating, they are often shocked that their minds are so full of thoughts. But nothing has changed; it's just that, before they meditated, they were so tied up with their thinking they couldn't even see it was there.

In meditation, we also begin to realise that our thoughts may not be an accurate reflection of what's going on in our lives – they can trip us up, telling us things that aren't true. How many times have you jumped to a conclusion, only to find out later on that you were wrong? Is there someone whom you took an instant dislike to at first, maybe because they reminded you of someone who mistreated you in the past, only to find that as you got to know them you actually had a lot in common? Maybe you'd be surprised if a man in a suit mugged you on the street, or if a youth in a hoodie held open the door for you?

By recognising that our perceptions can be wrong, distorted by our mental projections, we are starting to use a part of our minds that can go beyond our habitual assumptions and help us observe situations more accurately. We can begin to see things for what they are, not for what we think they are.

The next time you practise mindfulness of breathing or body, see if you can be curious about the relationship between your thoughts and your mind. As each new thought comes into your consciousness, notice how it arises, apparently from nowhere, passes through and then dissolves, soon to be replaced by another thought. Notice that there is another part of your mind which isn't any of those thoughts, which can experience them and watch them, but which doesn't have to identify with them, judge them or give them energy. Now ask yourself, 'If I am able to watch my thoughts, then are my thoughts really my mind? Indeed, are my thoughts really *me*?'

META-COGNITION

Western psychology calls the ability to reflect on our thoughts *meta-cognition*. Meta-cognition is crucial for mental health. We may not be able to do much about what our thoughts tell us – they seem to keep whirring away regardless of any attempts we make to stop them. But we *can* become skilled at choosing when to listen, and when to treat them as harmless background noise. We can stop buying into them, stop solidifying them into facts about ourselves and the world, and start to see them for what they are – just thoughts! We can decide to cultivate the 40 per cent of our mind that we can influence, rather than always listening to the 60 per cent that is stuck in the past.

Meta-cognition is the part of our consciousness that can act as a light – illuminating our world like the sun. The sun is constantly present, even when its light is obscured by the weather, or by the turning of the earth. Its radiance and warmth help us to relax, soften tense muscles and open our minds. It allows us to see things as they are and it lights up the world – the whole of our experience. It doesn't choose where to shed its light – it offers a completely non-judgemental perspective. It shines on good and bad with equal measure, on the living and the dying, on hunger and greed, on poverty and wealth, on peace and war. It is not discriminating – it simply shows us what is there. By learning how to use this aspect of our mind, we can watch our thoughts, feelings and bodily sensations, as well as the events in our lives, with awareness.

PRACTICE: Mindfulness of Mind – The Castle in the Sun

This practice can help us put thoughts in perspective. Instead of allowing them to dominate our experience, we see thoughts as simply part of an ever-changing landscape that includes our bodies (the castle), our thoughts (clouds), and the part of our mind that can shine a light on all the other aspects of experience – our awareness (the sun).

STEP ONE
First, settle yourself into mindfulness of breathing, using the first two steps as described in Chapter 2. Allow yourself a few minutes for each of the steps – paying attention to body posture and your breath in turn.

STEP TWO
Expand your attention from the breath out to your body as a whole. As you hold it in awareness, see if you can visualise your body as a magnificent castle, stood high up on a hill. Cultivate the sense that your body is strong like this castle, with its foundations laid deep in the earth – it is rock-solid, majestic, fit for a king or queen.

STEP THREE
Next, shift attention to the part of your mind that illuminates the scene. Visualise your awareness as a bright sun in daytime. From the sky of your mind, it shows you what's happening without judgement or distortion.

STEP FOUR
Now move your attention to your thoughts. Thoughts are like clouds passing across the sky of your mind, floating past the castle high on the hill. Some may be dark and ominous, others light and fluffy. The sky can be totally covered with them, or there might be just one or two wispy streaks across the horizon. These clouds are constantly changing shape and appearance as they pass by, eventually disappearing over the horizon. Sometimes

the sun is so powerful that its light can dissolve the clouds by shining on them, and simply placing our awareness on our thoughts is enough to show us they are not so solid – sometimes it seems weaker and our thoughts more persistent, and when there are heavy skies we might get so lost in our thoughts we forget it's there at all. But even at night, when the castle is temporarily in darkness, the sun is never far away.

STEP FIVE
Finally, take in the whole scene together: the castle, the sun, the clouds. By looking at this big picture, can you see how your body, your thoughts and your awareness relate to one another? Can you see that while all of these factors form aspects of our experience, they are none of them the whole of who we are? We are not just our body, not just our thoughts, and not even just our awareness. Rest your attention on this scene for as long as you like, watching the naturally ever-changing show in the light of your mind.

This exercise can be useful whenever we sense we are getting thoughts out of perspective. By seeing them as clouds floating across the sky, we are reminding ourselves that our experience is made up of more than just our thoughts – we can ground ourselves in our bodies, and use the light of our awareness to get a clearer picture of what is going on. You could practise it for a few minutes during mindfulness of breathing or body, or at any moment in your day when you feel overwhelmed. You don't always have to be sitting down – you could just close your eyes and flash your mind straight onto Step Five..

Developing our meta-cognition is a key part of most psychotherapies, including cognitive therapy, which is becoming increasingly widely available in the UK. By encouraging people to become more aware of how their habitual thought processes are sometimes inaccurate, outdated or unhelpful, cognitive therapists point out that we can ignore or change our thoughts when what they tell us isn't based in reality.

Let's take depression, one of the most common mental health problems. When we get depressed, most of us find ourselves having negative thoughts about ourselves, our lives and the world around us. We think about bad things that have happened and feel hopeless about the future. Our thinking reinforces our state of mind and is full of self-criticism and pessimism. 'Why do these things always happen to me?', 'I'm useless when it comes to handling problems,' 'It's always the same – nothing ever seems to change – I'm never going to get better.' We allow our thinking to 'beat us up' and reinforce the way we feel.

Unfortunately, if we believe those kinds of thoughts, they actually perpetuate our depression – we start feeling bad about feeling bad, even once the problems that triggered the depression have passed. It's the Buddha's second arrow of suffering again – if being unhappy wasn't enough, we start blaming ourselves for our unhappiness, reinforcing our sense of inadequacy and our lack of control, and this keeps us depressed. The problem seems to get worse the more times we get depressed – research suggests that later episodes of depression can be triggered simply by negative thinking, even when there hasn't been any major crisis to set it off. This may be partly how and why depression becomes a chronic, recurrent condition.[10]

The first challenge for a cognitive therapist working with a depressed person is to help the person see that his or her negative thoughts and perceptions are sometimes inaccurate – to notice how, under stress, the mind interprets everything through the distorted mirror of our projections, making things look worse than they actually are. When we learn that we don't have to believe everything our minds are telling us, we are developing meta-cognition – we can start to distance ourselves from negative thoughts, not be so dominated by them and begin to release the powerful grip they have on our lives. We don't have to take our thoughts so personally. If we can do this, our negative thoughts will stop being all-consuming and, slowly, we can begin to work our way out of the depression.

But it's one thing to understand intellectually that negative thoughts keep us depressed, and quite another to actually let go of destructive mental patterns that we've been practising all our lives. We are trying to use our mind to change our mind – and that's not easy! To manage it, we need a way of separating out the thoughts that are giving us so much grief from the bigger, more spacious, meta-cognitive mind which can hold those thoughts in kindly awareness, and which doesn't have to buy into what they try to tell us. This is exactly what mindfulness training offers. By slowing down, noticing our thoughts in a friendly manner and choosing not to feed those that are unhelpful, we can gradually develop a healthier way of using our minds. Mindfulness strengthens our 'meta-cognitive muscles'.

TREATMENTS FOR DEPRESSION

Jon Kabat-Zinn's work with people experiencing chronic physical health problems soon came to the attention of experts working to help people with mental health issues. In the mid-1990s, the stress-reduction clinic at the University of Massachusetts hosted a series of visits from Mark Williams and John Teasdale from Cambridge University, and Zindel Segal from Toronto's Clarke Institute of Psychiatry. Williams, Teasdale and Segal are cognitive psychologists who were working to develop treatments for depression. They had been asked to develop a new group version of cognitive therapy, aimed specifically at helping people who had been depressed several times. They were especially looking for ways that people could be taught psychological techniques that would help them ward off another episode.

The three had decided to focus on the problem of 'negative thinking'. They had heard about Jon Kabat-Zinn through a colleague, and realised that his mindfulness instructions – showing patients how to stop fighting their experience and just observe it instead – might be just what depressed people needed. If there were a set of practices that people could learn and which could help them not to buy into their negative thoughts, perhaps they too could be released from some of their stress?

One of the difficulties that cognitive therapists have when working with depressed people is that it isn't always easy for them to create enough space between their thoughts and their mind to really *see* that thoughts are not facts. When we are depressed, our minds can feel so tight that it seems almost like we are suffocating – in this state, our thoughts can be so overwhelming that it is almost impossible to accept that they are not quite as 'real' as they seem.

If we are completely tied up with our thinking like this, it is difficult to develop meta-cognition, and trying to challenge thoughts, as cognitive therapy encourages, can actually set us up for a distressing internal battle. Instead of being more positive, we may end up criticising ourselves, perhaps aggressively blaming our minds for not being more cheerful or trying to suppress negative thoughts altogether, and then becoming even more depressed when we realise that this doesn't work. It's the same problem that patients in chronic pain have with their bodies: fighting pain, or trying to avoid it, can actually make it worse. We are just ramping up the suffering and firing even more arrows at ourselves.

The struggle is even more of a problem when we are depressed, because depression brings with it a tendency to 'ruminate'. This means we churn over and over in our minds why we have got depressed and what we should do about it, worrying endlessly about our situation. Unfortunately, thinking more and more about depression like this makes it worse rather than better. We just become more and more preoccupied, introspective and focused on our (unhappy) selves, feeding our misery and making it grow. Then, of course, we ruminate even more. It's a vicious circle.

It is also very speedy. We may feel sluggish, lethargic and slow when we are depressed, but internally we may be paralysed by our racing minds. The obsessive rumination

that comes with depression is another example of
overactivity – only this time occurring on a mental level. Our
minds get faster and faster as we try to think our way out of
our problems, even though this actually plunges us further
into depression. So, we become more and more exhausted,
more and more stressed, and more and more depressed.

Segal, Williams and Teasdale wondered whether
mindfulness practice could help depressed people let go of
rumination. By watching thoughts in meditation, without
getting caught up in them, perhaps people who were
depressed might stop digging themselves further into their
hole? The psychologists' visits to the stress-reduction clinic
gave them cause for optimism. Observing the mindfulness-
based stress-reduction programme, they saw ordinary
people with chronic health problems learning how to
deal with pain in an entirely new and often life-changing
fashion, just by using their minds in a different way.

As respected scientists, the psychologists had some
worries about what their 'no-nonsense' colleagues
might think about them trying something as apparently
flaky as meditation for a condition as intractable as
depression. Mark Williams remembers being accosted by
an incredulous colleague at a conference and asked: 'Is it
really true what I hear, that you are *meditating* with your
patients?' But to their credit, the psychologists decided to
trust the evidence, the testimonies of patients and staff at
the U Mass Medical School and their own eyes and ears.
For the next several years they dedicated themselves to
adapting the stress-reduction programme for people with
depression.

The new treatment, Mindfulness-Based Cognitive Therapy (MBCT), retained all the main elements of MBSR, but also introduced some tools and techniques from cognitive therapy, specifically designed for people at risk of depression. These included role-play exercises to show how negative thinking can make moods worse, and asking participants to write individual relapse-prevention plans to put in place when they spot the early warning signs of a relapse.

Although it was meant for people with a 'mental' health problem, MBCT retained the strong emphasis that MBSR puts on paying attention to the body. People who are depressed tend to get so tied up with their thoughts that they lose touch with their bodies. Despite the name we give them, mental health problems don't just happen in the head – people who are depressed experience lots of physical symptoms such as chest pains, heart palpitations, headaches, muscle tension and back pain, a churning stomach, constipation, tiredness, sleep disturbance and poor appetite.

When we practise mindfulness, we are training ourselves to stay grounded in our bodies *and* our minds. It's a way of working with problems based not on obsessively, speedily thinking our way out, but on paying attention to the whole of our experience – body sensations, feelings *and* thoughts. When we are mindfully aware of our entire experience in this way, there is a greater chance of being able to spot the warning signs of depression – a tightness in the shoulders perhaps, a sense that our thoughts are beginning to race, a realisation that we are avoiding seeing friends, or an awareness that we are tending to respond to situations with increasing negativity. By training ourselves to use the mind in a mindful way, we are giving ourselves the best chance of noticing the signs of oncoming stress, and taking steps to prevent it from escalating into depression, or whatever other destructive mind states we are prone to.

SCIENTIFIC TESTING

Like Jon Kabat-Zinn, the psychologists knew that to have a hope of persuading a sceptical medical establishment that their treatment could be effective, they had to test it scientifically. Did mindfulness-based cognitive therapy actually help people at risk of falling into depression to stay well? To find out, they carried out a trial, conducted jointly at their universities in Toronto, Cambridge and Bangor (Mark Williams had by this time moved from Cambridge to North Wales).[11] They randomly allocated 145 patients at high risk of depression to one of two groups, and put one group through a course of mindfulness-based cognitive therapy, while the others carried on receiving their usual treatment. The progress of the two sets of patients was then measured over the following year.

The results were clear: of the patients who had suffered more than two episodes of depression (three-quarters of those in the trial), just over a third who received MBCT relapsed over the next 12 months. But for similar patients who had not received MBCT, the relapse rate was twice as high – two-thirds became depressed again. Offering MBCT to those patients who were most prone to depression had made a significant difference – their chances of staying well in the year after the course had doubled.

In 2004, a second similar trial produced even more positive results.[12] This time around, 36 per cent of the MBCT participants relapsed, compared to 78 per cent for the group that did not learn any mindfulness techniques. MBCT was a resounding success.

Following these two studies, Mindfulness-Based Cognitive Therapy received an important endorsement. In the UK, a body called the National Institute for Health and Clinical Excellence (NICE) decides, based on the best available scientific evidence, which treatments should be offered on the National Health Service. Following the MBCT trials, NICE recommended the new treatment's use for people who have suffered more than two episodes of depression.

Offering meditation to help people prone to depression was now official NHS policy. Within just a few short years of being developed, mindfulness-based cognitive therapy had become a government-approved treatment for depression, alongside more well-established medical approaches such as anti-depressant drugs and psychological therapies such as CBT (cognitive behavioural therapy). Meditation was no longer on the fringes of medicine – an 'alternative' approach scorned by hardcore scientists. Segal, Williams and Teasdale's work had been endorsed at the highest level – mindfulness had gone mainstream.

KATHY'S EXPERIENCE

Kathy, 47, was referred for mindfulness-based cognitive therapy three years ago. She says

mindfulness has been the missing piece in her mental health jigsaw ...

Kathy has a long history of depression. About 12 years ago she was prescribed medication, and the drugs seemed to bring her some stability. As she gradually improved, she talked with her GP about finding new ways to cope. Her doctor referred her to a cognitive behavioural therapist, and she also went to see a nutritionist.

One day she was chatting with a friend in the US who mentioned mindfulness training – the friend raved about how much she had benefited from it. Kathy lives in Oxford, one of the places in the UK where MBCT is available on the NHS. So when Kathy mentioned mindfulness to her therapist, she could refer her onto a course.

At the first session, the teacher led the group in a 'body scan'. Kathy immediately thought: 'Yes, I can do this!' 'That doesn't mean it was easy,' she adds. 'It was quite a challenge to make time to do the practice every day. But it felt like something I could manage.' And slowly but surely, as the weeks went by, Kathy began to feel something changing for her. 'I started to be able to recognise more of my own issues – particularly my tendency to want to *do everything right*. It was quite painful to see it come up during the meditation sessions, but I really felt something shifting in me.'

It wasn't long before Kathy really began to feel the benefits of her training. 'Towards the end of the course, or it might have been just afterwards, I took a Saturday morning continuing education class. For the first time in one of those classes, I really felt I could *be there* mentally. I wasn't feeling guilty for not doing something else, like staying at home with my family. Mindfulness has given me the ability to feel more connected – to more fully *be* wherever I am. One of my kids asked me why I was doing the course and I said I was learning how to pay attention. They thought it was really stupid, but that sums it up for me – you're learning how to recognise what's going on, internally and externally.'

MBCT has had a big impact on how Kathy handles her moods. 'I've got my medication down as low as it's ever been and I haven't had a major depression since the course. Unpleasant feelings and stress still come, but I'm not engaging with them like I used to. If I get delayed when I really need to be somewhere else, I don't waste all my energy worrying about it – I can say: "OK, I'm here now, so let's make the most of it." And I'm more OK when I've had a really stressful week.'

A good example of how practising mindfulness helps Kathy came when she and her family went to London for some Christmas shopping. 'We were in a big toy department and it was really busy,' she remembers. 'I don't usually do crowds well – I don't like the pressure and stress. I started getting anxious about losing one of the kids – I basically had a kind of panic attack. But I know that when things get hard, I need to pay attention to what my body is doing. So, I started saying to myself: "OK, my heart rate and blood pressure are going up, I am feeling very tense and my shoulders are tightening." Just that process helped me to back up a little bit – I didn't go into a full panic attack, even though I had been verging on it. I think if I hadn't had the mindfulness training to help me think a bit differently, I probably wouldn't have been able to ward it off. Being able to recognise experiences in my body is enough to stop me getting sucked into my old patterns, blaming and judging myself.'

Like most of us, Kathy leads a busy life and has lots of responsibilities. But although having a family to look after doesn't leave her with a lot of spare time, she knows that she needs to continue training her mind to keep it in the best shape. 'A little bit of practice every day makes a huge amount of difference,' she says.

Kathy had tried lots of different ways of coping with depression – many of them helpful. But she says MBCT has made the most difference. 'I've done a lot of talk therapy, but mindfulness has made the bigger shift, probably because of the way it helps you pay attention and take that step back. For me at least, depression comes from getting overwhelmed with pain or frustration or irritability, and I'm not participating in those feelings the way I used to. I think mindfulness is the piece that's missing in other kinds of psychotherapy.'

The scientific evidence for MBCT has continued to amass. In 2007, a team led by Professor Willem Kuyken at Exeter University carried out another trial which showed that mindfulness compares well with the most commonly used treatment for people with depression – anti-depressant drugs.[13] Kuyken and his colleagues followed 123 people who had a history of recurrent depression and had been taking anti-depressants as a 'maintenance' treatment. That means they had continued to be prescribed drugs long term, even when they were no longer depressed, in the hope that the anti-depressant would offer a chemical boost that would stop them relapsing. The patients were either given MBCT (in which case they were also encouraged to come off anti-depressants) or asked to continue as usual with their anti-depressants.

In the year following the course, 60 per cent of the non-MBCT group relapsed, compared to 47 per cent of those who were taught mindfulness (three-quarters of whom *also* stopped taking anti-depressants). Not only was MBCT better at preventing relapse, according to the researchers, but it was also more likely to improve the participants' quality of life. To top it all, MBCT was more cost-effective than anti-depressants over the period of the trial, with the likelihood that the savings would be even greater over a longer period of time. This is because meditation techniques don't usually have to be 're-prescribed' – patients can continue to practise at home, after the course is over, taking charge of their own mental health rather than relying on pills. And, of course, while anti-depressants can have nasty side effects, mindfulness has lots of *positive* side effects: all the benefits to physical health and stress reduction that we explored in the last chapter, not to mention the potential for enjoying greater body–mind wholeness, the ability to manifest more completely in our speedy, disintegrated world, and a growing ability to simply '*be*' that balances our tendency towards overactivity.

There have now been several small trials offering mindfulness-based cognitive therapy to people when they are actually depressed, rather than when they are in between episodes. The early results from these are encouraging – in one study, MBCT reduced people's symptoms of depression from severe to mild (compared to no change in a group who didn't receive the treatment), while another found that a third of patients were no longer depressed at the end of the course.[14] Mindfulness-based treatments have also been used successfully for people with other mental health problems, including borderline personality disorder, obsessive-compulsive disorder, and social phobia.[15]

Unfortunately, this isn't quite the happy end of the story that it might seem. For while mindfulness-based cognitive therapy has received official endorsement, that doesn't mean that everyone who might benefit is likely to be offered a place on a course. In 2009, five years after the NICE recommendation, Ed led a project at the Mental Health Foundation designed to find out how much GPs knew about mindfulness, and how often they followed the NICE guidelines.[16] The results were simultaneously heartening and disappointing.

GPS AND MINDFULNESS

The heartening part was that GPs were very positive about the potential for mindfulness to benefit their patients – the scientific evidence seems to have done its job at persuading doctors. In fact, a massive 72 per cent of GPs said they thought it would be helpful for their patients with mental health problems to learn mindfulness meditation (69 per cent also thought it would be useful for their patients in general). This is even more remarkable when you consider that most of the rest (22 per cent) hadn't yet heard of mindfulness-based cognitive therapy. GPs were actually so keen on mindfulness that two-thirds (64 per cent) wanted to receive training in it themselves.

More frustrating, however, was the realisation that GPs' enthusiasm for mindfulness was unlikely to have much impact on the people who really need the treatment – their patients. Only one in 20 GPs said they referred their patients to MBCT 'very often', and more than two-thirds said they rarely or never did so. This probably isn't GPs' fault: only a fifth have access to courses they can direct their patients to. While there are some areas of the UK where mindfulness courses are taught quite regularly (such as Devon, Oxford, North Wales and some parts of Scotland), there are many other places where the chances of being referred onto a course are very small, even if you or your GP has heard of and is positive about the approach.

As Jonty and every other GP knows only too well, the need for something to help people who experience recurrent depression is huge. They are often regulars at their local surgery, and once they have tried drugs or therapy, their doctors usually have little to offer them. In the Mental Health Foundation survey, 93 per cent of GPs said they wanted more effective treatment options for people who repeatedly get depressed.

MBCT makes good financial sense, too – as well as being more cost-effective than anti-depressants, MBCT may well be less expensive than other psychotherapies. Mindfulness can be taught in large groups – a course of MBCT takes around five hours of a therapist's time per patient, compared to around 16 hours – more than three times as much – for a typical course of cognitive therapy. And there could be a wider benefit, too – by reducing the rate of relapse among people who get depressed a lot, they are likely to go to the doctor less often, be more able to hold down jobs and maintain successful relationships, and so contribute more to the economy and to society.

Mindfulness isn't just relevant to the mental health of people who are experiencing 'problems' – it can help any of us who want to look after our minds better. Couldn't most of us benefit from slowing down, putting our thoughts into perspective and bringing our minds and bodies into balance? Who can say they never get tied up with their own thoughts, identifying with them in a way that leads to action that they might later regret? However mentally healthy or mindful we think we are already, wouldn't we feel better if we were able to practise 'noticing' – being curious, catching sight of the beautiful and savouring the moment?

DIXON'S EXPERIENCE

When Dixon signed up for a mindfulness-based cognitive therapy course, he hoped to learn techniques to help him deal with his tendency towards depression. He did – but mindfulness has helped him cope with a lot more than just his low moods…

Dixon, now in his mid-fifties, has suffered from depression since he was a teenager, but he says his difficulties really came to the fore after he had Q fever – an illness caused by a bacterial infection with symptoms similar to severe flu, and which also affects the liver. 'From then on,' he says, 'my health was never the same.' Also diagnosed with Chronic Fatigue Syndrome, Dixon soldiered on working as a teacher, but says he was often depressed and tired.

Then his doctor suggested a course of mindfulness-based cognitive therapy. At first, Dixon was sceptical. 'If I'd been asked about meditation before that, I'd have remembered my youth and the Beatles and thought: "Yes, well, that's OK for a bunch of long-haired hippies, but it's not for me!'" But he decided he had nothing to lose. 'I thought: "Well, let's give it a go – the worst that can happen is you go along a couple of times and if everyone's burning joss sticks and wearing kaftans, you can walk away." But it wasn't like that.'

Dixon says that MBCT gave him both an understanding of depression and the tools to deal with it. 'I learned how depression affects people like me, and how to recognise the problems before they become serious. Depression consists of the mind wandering into areas that it shouldn't go, either reviewing painful or unpleasant things from the past or considering fears for the future. With practice you become aware of what your mind is doing – you notice: "Oh yes, I'm thinking about something that I don't need to be thinking about. That's a terrific weapon against depression."

'Once you have a regular meditation practice, you can say: "I'm in charge of my life." I know that sounds strange but I don't think I was before. I wasn't in charge of my mind – it went and did its own thing, and I wasn't aware that I was recycling a lot of stuff and making myself very anxious and worried. Depression makes people focus on themselves and their own problems to the point that they stop functioning. Mindfulness stops you from doing that. It stops you from allowing your mind to tie you up.'

Two years ago, Dixon's mindfulness training became even more relevant. He was admitted to hospital with severe back pain, and doctors told him he had bone cancer – he had three shattered vertebrae as a result of the cancer eroding his spine. He now uses the 'mental tools' he learned on the MBCT course to deal with the pain, disability and challenges of living with a serious physical illness.

'When I did the course', he explains, 'I had no inkling of the fact that I had other medical issues, but mindfulness has helped a lot in coping with pain. Through meditation you examine the nature of pain and discomfort and get up close to it – you find out about it. And surprisingly, the closer you get the more you are able to deal with it. If I have pains in my lower back or my pelvis I can sit there and pay attention to it – surprisingly often, you realise the pain isn't as dreadful as you thought. We think that hurting is hurting, but it's how you perceive it. A lot of pain is down to what's in your mind. That's quite strange – five years ago if somebody had said that to me I'd have been like: "Cobblers! If it hurts, it hurts!"'

Dixon has recently had major surgery to repair his spine, chemotherapy and a stem cell transplant – when he was in hospital, he would sit on his bed and use the mindfulness practices he learned on the course, and he prioritises them when he's at home, usually managing to practise for about half an hour, four times a week. 'I'm not only dealing with depression now,' he explains. 'I'm also dealing with all the fears that go with a serious, long-term illness. Meditation helps me calm my mind and focus and make sure that I don't panic or over-react. It's helped me to come to terms with the problem that I've got and how to deal with it.

'By focusing on the here and now, you're dealing not with the fear about "What's going to happen to my family?" and all the other things that weigh you down, but "How are things right at this moment?" That's a wonderful thing to be able to do – a lifeline. My son is 11 years old and he needs a dad who can take him to his football training and tell jokes – MBCT has given me the courage and fortitude to do that. It sets my mind up to crack on with life rather than sinking into a swamp of despondency.'

BEING YOUR OWN GOOD PARENT

Another helpful way of thinking about mindfulness of mind is as a kind of 'self-parenting'. By learning how to develop a non-critical 'observing' part of our consciousness and using it to watch, hold and be kind to our thoughts and feelings, no matter how difficult they become, we are actually looking after our thoughts just like a good mother or father looks after a child – with love, patience, compassion and flexibility. By practising mindfulness of mind, we are offering firm and wise guidance to our thoughts when they tell us something unhelpful – to panic or give up, perhaps – and we are doing this from a place of kindness, not criticism.

Psychologists have long said that a child needs this kind of firm but loving guidance to grow up into a psychologically healthy adult, at which point he can carry on the guiding process for himself. A child who gets this kind of attention from her caregivers develops what is known as 'secure attachment' – she learns to trust the world around her, and, as she grows up, to trust herself. 'Securely attached' people feel confident about trying new experiences, making friends and dealing with life's inevitable setbacks. To be fundamentally happy, they are not dependent on the opinion of others, or for everything always to go well in their lives. These are all the hallmarks of good mental health.

On the other hand, if a child doesn't get this kind of care, support and attention, he may never learn to feel safe and comforted, or to know how to regulate his thoughts, feelings and behaviour. He may be unable to look after himself, and feel frightened, lonely and under-confident a lot of the time. He may lack good boundaries, and live a chaotic life. He may have a 'fragile ego', always needing other people to like him, worried that something bad is going to happen or that he won't be able to cope on his own. Insecurely attached people have never learned to internalise a 'good parent' because they did not experience good parenting as a child.

By learning mindfulness practices, which seem gradually to help us grow our own internal 'good parent', we may be more readily able to offer this sort of kindly, strong and loving support to ourselves (and, therefore, others) at any time, even if we did not receive so much of it when we were younger.

Attachment theory was developed by a British psychiatrist called John Bowlby in the mid-20th century – it certainly wasn't around in the time of the Buddha. But interestingly, the image of mindfulness practice as being like a compassionate parent looking after a frightened child also appears in some Buddhist-based teachings, which speak of 'placing the mind of fearfulness in the cradle of loving-kindness'.[17] How often can any of us say that we are this compassionate towards our own minds?

If mindfulness practices really do help create 'secure attachment', they could give people the skills which come naturally to more securely attached people – the confidence to function well in and enjoy the world around them, to find meaningful occupations, keep learning new things, develop mutually satisfying relationships with friends and family, and be kind and considerate to others.

Researchers have noted the uncanny similarities between the desirable qualities possessed by people who are 'securely attached' and those who are naturally mindful.[18] Naturally mindful people (those who, in tests, have been shown to possess a high degree of what psychologists call 'trait' or 'dispositional' mindfulness) are not only less likely to suffer psychological distress, including depression and anxiety, but they are less neurotic, more extrovert, more satisfied with their lives and enjoy a greater sense of wellbeing. They have more awareness, understanding and acceptance of their emotions, and are less likely to react impulsively to them.

More naturally mindful people also recover from bad moods more quickly, ruminate less, are less likely to shy away from difficult experiences and aren't as perfectionist. They have fewer negative thoughts and are less likely to get hung up on them. And they have greater self-esteem that is less dependent on things going well in their lives – they are not shattered by stress, and know what to do to look after themselves when they are under pressure. Put simply, they have better mental health, more emotional intelligence, and live more contented lives.

As we have shown, there is now substantial scientific evidence that by training in mindfulness, people can learn how to become happier – its effects can be demonstrated on the body, in the brain, through clinical trials and through people's own reported experience. It is also inexpensive to teach, simple to learn and practise, and gives people the tools to work with their own minds, at a time when our health services are overwhelmed by more mental health problems (not to mention, as we saw in Chapter 3, stress-related physical health problems) than they are equipped to handle. To top all that, mindfulness provides a powerful antidote to the anxiety-producing, health-draining forces of speed and overactivity that assail our minds from every angle in our stressed-out society.

MENTAL FLOSS

Mindfulness is basic mind hygiene – it can do for your mental health what brushing your teeth does for your dental health. Most of us don't even think twice about brushing our teeth every day – we learn from an early age that if we don't want tooth decay, brushing is essential. Of course, there are other things we can do to look after our teeth, too – regular visits to the dentist and hygienist, flossing, cutting out sugary foods and drinks. But without brushing as our central daily practice, we're still likely to end up with rotten teeth and bad breath. We brush because we have been trained to do so and because we understand what will happen if we don't.

But is neglecting your teeth really worse than neglecting your mental health? Isn't it strange that we pay more daily attention to caring for the enamel on our teeth than we do listening to and tuning our mind? Even if we spent just 15 minutes practising mindfulness of mind at the start of each day, we might soon become far better equipped to skilfully handle all the incoming data that is thrown at us during the rest of the next 24 hours. When the benefits of mindfulness meditation are so readily accessible, and so wide-ranging, is there any reason why we shouldn't all be encouraged to train in it as part of our ongoing health education, just as we all learn how important it is to look after our teeth?

MINDFULNESS OF MIND: SUGGESTIONS FOR WORKING WITH THOUGHTS

DON'T TRY TO STOP THINKING

There's a common myth that meditation means having a blank mind, or trying to stop your thoughts. But thoughts are not the enemy – trying to stop them will just lead to more struggle. Mindfulness of mind means observing your experience as it is, thoughts included.

FEELING OVERWHELMED BY THOUGHTS

You may feel like you have a lot of thoughts in your mind when you start practising mindfulness. It can be a bit like coming off a merry-go-round. At first, we feel dizzy, but that's because we've suddenly stopped spinning. When we sit down to meditate, we are dropping our busyness, and it may feel like our minds are even more crazy than usual. In fact, we are just noticing our habitual speed – we are becoming more aware.

NOT JUDGING THOUGHTS

In meditation, there are no 'good' and no 'bad' thoughts – there are just thoughts. Cultivate an attitude of equanimity to whatever goes through your mind when you meditate – see if you can watch your thoughts with interest, without fighting them, being judgemental of them, or attaching to them.

ACCEPTING THAT THE MIND GETS CAUGHT UP IN THOUGHTS

It is tempting to criticise ourselves when our awareness wanders away from the object of meditation and gets tied up in thoughts. But this happens to everyone – it's part of the practice. Mind-wandering is an opportunity to be patient – no matter how many times your mind strays, you just keep on bringing it back, gently and calmly. That IS mindfulness meditation.

Jonty's Experience

Whilst I would not consider myself to have a 'mental health problem', if you ask anyone who knows me they will tell you that I am a bit of a worrier! I am also a perfectionist (the two seem to go hand in hand!). These traits have been with me for a very long time and, depending on whom you ask, may be related to a need for approval or simply the fact that I am a Virgo! Why I am the way I am is interesting (at least to me!) and I have spent some time with a therapist exploring these things. However, what seems more important in many ways is how I relate to these characteristics and what impact they have on my life right *now*. For me they have always felt destructive – constantly trying to do so much and having to keep on top of so many different things feels stressful – like being constantly afraid of dropping something. However, for my patients these could be seen as good qualities in their doctor – the last thing any of us wants is a doctor who forgets us, doesn't check on our results or delays referring us to the hospital.

Mindfulness has, first and foremost, allowed me to see more clearly what drives me. As a process of introspection it has helped me to identify and take ownership of my role in the stress I feel. Like many of my patients, I tend to focus on what is making me feel worried or unhappy in my life, and try to work out how to change that: perhaps I need to alter my working week, perhaps I should see more of my friends, perhaps I should stop writing this book (!), perhaps I even need a new job … All of these things may, of course, be true, and I have certainly contemplated them all at one time or another, but what is also important is to remember that my *perception* of my situation is contributing to how I feel. Mindfulness helps me notice my own contribution to my stress and work with it – not with blame or criticism – but in an interested and accepting way. This allows me to acknowledge my role and try and deal more clearly with the reality of the situation, rather than being driven by my automatic responses to stress and simply looking to blame others for the way I feel.

Ed's Experience

I remember clearly the day a psychotherapist first told me to 'observe my experience'. I took the bus back home and, putting her advice into practice, suddenly became aware that it was possible to look at the workings of my mind from an outsider's perspective. I could watch myself getting on the bus and walking up to the top deck, and then notice myself looking at the people walking by on the street below. Most importantly, I could watch my mind having thoughts about each of these experiences without necessarily being caught up in what I was thinking. This was a revelation to me – I didn't know it at the time, but it was my first conscious experience of meditation, and of 'meta-cognition'.

A year or two later, after some months of practising mindfulness, I noticed that I was able to click into this mode more often. And the next time I became depressed, I was able to relate to the experience in a very different way. Yes, I still felt in pain; yes, my mind was still racing; and yes, my thoughts were still spinning through the most negative scenarios possible. But I no longer had to be an active participant in all of that – I could disengage from the depression and just notice all of its qualities – however unpleasant they were. This had the effect of reducing its sting as well as stopping me from adding fuel to its fire – rather than agreeing with the thoughts that told me: 'This will never end' or 'I am totally useless,' I could let those ruminations motor through my mind and see them as false perceptions rather than objective truths.

I wouldn't want to give the impression that practising mindfulness makes depression easy to cope with – it certainly doesn't – but I do know that my own episodes have become shorter and less frequent since I've been practising. Just as a wound on the skin heals more quickly if you don't pick at it, so depression seems to pass more quickly if I am kind to myself rather than getting even more irritated. It sounds counter-intuitive, but for me depression seems to go away more quickly if I make friends with it.

CHAPTER FIVE

MINDFULNESS OF FEELINGS

Work mindfully with your emotions and you can loosen the bonds of addiction that limit life. The more we are mindful of our feelings, the more we can open up to the miracle of the moment.

Remember what the Buddha said about the cause of our suffering? We're so determined to escape the pain of life, and so desperate for pleasure, that we get drawn into self-defeating behaviours that make us *more* unhappy. The Buddha said this was the second noble truth – clinging. These days, we often call it addiction.

We're not just talking here about addiction to alcohol or drugs. Addiction is everywhere in our over-active world, and it's usually an attempt to control how we feel. For some of us it's working late to distract ourselves from our loneliness; for others it's going to the gym to try and stave off the ageing of our bodies. Some people get a buzz from the piece of chocolate cake they have with their coffee, or from speeding on the motorway, or putting money on horses. Maybe you're addicted to lying under the duvet for as long as you can each morning, or to getting the sun tan that you think brings appreciation from potential lovers? Or perhaps you are attached to zoning out in front of the TV, or having your tea made with just the right amount of milk?

It's not that going to the gym, having a lie-in, eating chocolate cake or even drinking alcohol are necessarily bad things to do. The problem comes when we engage in these activities compulsively, in a bid to manipulate our experience. That's when we can end up causing ourselves harm. Psychologist John Bradshaw's definition of addiction is 'a pathological relationship to any mood-altering experience that has life-damaging consequences'. According to this definition, we are addicted any time we keep doing something that is supposed to make us feel better, but which actually ends up hurting us.[1]

Let's take an obvious example: smoking cigarettes. Cigarettes provide a short-term relief from anxiety. The inhalation of nicotine into the body, the infantile comfort of sucking on the filter, the relief of having something to do with the hands and mouth – all of these actions create small distractions from whatever is troubling the smoker, whether it's nerves before a job interview, the boredom of waiting at a bus stop, or some nagging existential doubt (Why am I here? Where is my life going?).

But the strategy doesn't work so well in the long term. We can't escape from anxiety so easily – uncertainty and change are part of life, and that frightens us. Cigarettes might temporarily distract us from our fear, but the costs are enormous. Smokers massively increase their risk of heart disease, emphysema, lung cancer and a whole range of other unpleasant illnesses. Each cigarette acts as a short-lived smokescreen from the discomforts of the moment, but it also hastens some of the things we get most anxious about – it brings illness and death ever closer. Yet despite all the warnings, one in four of us keeps on puffing – in the UK, 120,000 people die each year from tobacco-related diseases.[2]

Of course, you may not be a smoker – perhaps you gave up long ago, or never started. That's great, but can you really say your life is free of the same addictive patterns when it comes to other activities? Do you have no reassuring little habits that you use to create your own smokescreen from your feelings? What about alcohol? One in three men and one in five women regularly drinks more than the recommended limits, using booze to take the edge off their emotions, lulling themselves into a stupor at the end of the day.[3] Or shopping – each year we spend billions on consumer goods, often working at jobs we don't like so we can earn the money to pay for stuff that we think will satisfy us, but which leaves us feeling empty once the thrill of the purchase has worn off.

When we buy a new coat, is it really because we need something to protect ourselves from the cold, or because its warmth is a substitute for what we really want, perhaps a hug from a friend or partner? When, as teenagers, we sat engrossed in a computer game or watching TV for hours, was it because we really enjoyed it, or so that we didn't have to deal with our anxiety around meeting new people, or the rage we felt at our parents?

We can use almost any activity, any form of impulsive 'doing', to remove our attention from the painful feelings that are part and parcel of life. It could be sex, food, books, gossip or marijuana – whenever we indulge as a way to avoid the feelings of the present moment, we are acting out the second noble truth. As the American Buddhist nun Pema Chodron puts it, 'We use all kinds of things to escape – all addictions stem from this moment when we meet our edge and we just can't stand it.'[4]

Our avoidance strategies aren't always external ones – addictive patterns can also take place in the mind. In Chapter 4 we saw that people who get depressed are prone to 'rumination' – a kind of compulsive thinking that actually embeds depression ever further, even though it's meant to be a search for solutions. By ruminating, we avoid the pain of the present moment by obsessively focusing on the past or the future – it's an internally based addiction.

It's not just depressives that get stuck in their mental world – many of us learn to intellectualise our lives rather than experience them. This over-dependence on thinking can lead to the sort of half-life of rationality that afflicted Mr Spock in *Star Trek*, leaving us trapped in a prison of logic, unable to relate to anything that requires an emotional connection. People who are addicted to rationality might stand under the night sky and explain the physics of how the moon revolves around the Earth, but they can't really feel the magic of moonlight in their heart. Albert Einstein once said that there are two ways to live life – as though nothing is a miracle, and as though everything is a miracle. But you can't experience everything as a miracle if you are disconnected from your feelings.

We aren't pointing the finger. All of us are more or less addicted to something – as the Buddha saw, our self-defeating patterns of clinging to pleasure and avoiding pain are deeply ingrained. To some greater or lesser degree, almost everything we do is meant to comfort us, or make us feel less sad, frightened or frustrated. We all want to be happy. It's just that the strategies we use aren't quite what they're cracked up to be. And when we keep resorting to them, we never learn more effective coping skills that might help us manage our feelings and our situation more effectively. We get stuck in the same old vicious cycles.

So why don't we just stop? If compulsive shopping drains our finances and brings us a house full of junk, why don't we restrict ourselves to what we really need, and splash our cash on something that will actually make us feel good? Instead of buying ourselves another pair of shoes, why don't we treat a friend to dinner – a simple act of 'connecting' and 'giving' that would rack us up two portions of the five-a-day 'mental health diet' we talked about in the last chapter? Indeed, if we ride our bike to the restaurant, manage to stay present during the meal and choose a friend from whom we learn, then we'll have notched up everything we need to keep our mind in shape for the day.

Why do we instead often choose to drink, smoke, spend, shout, binge, think too much or work obsessively when they have such damaging consequences for us?

THE ANSWER IS THREEFOLD

First, we don't always *see* clearly what we are doing – unless we're aware that our addictive patterns are destructive, we'll have no reason to stop. Until the link between cigarettes and lung cancer was proven, there was far less awareness of the damage that tobacco could do to our health. People might have thought it was a dirty habit, but they didn't know it was going to kill them – and so a lot more people smoked.

It usually takes a heavy dose of awareness to convince us that we need to change our habits. Even with what we now know about the dangers of smoking, people still find justifications to continue: 'I'll give up in a few years, before it does any real damage,' 'My granddad smoked and he lived till he was 90,' 'I'm a risk-taker – I don't care if I die young, as long as I've had fun.'

It's the same with our other addictions – we say we drink because we like a party (not because we feel anxious in social situations), or we buy the most expensive clothes because we're stylish, not because wearing designer labels gives us the confidence we lack. We intellectualise because we think we're being smart, and we shout at others because we think they deserve it. We'll do almost anything to avoid painful feelings. The Buddha said that the very root cause of our suffering was ignorance or delusion. In Western psychology this is called *denial*.

Even when we *are* aware of what we're doing, it's not so easy to let go of our defences. Though they may be storing up more pain in the long run, our addictive behaviours do make us feel good – for a bit. Cigarettes *do* mask a bit of anxiety when you're smoking, just as driving a fast car *can* help you feel more alive and more powerful when you're hitting top speed on the motorway. When we drop our habitual patterns, we're suddenly exposed to the very feelings of fear, sadness, emptiness or rage that we've been trying to avoid. Letting go of our addictions means having to face our feelings, not in some distant future, but right here, right now. Ouch. No thanks.

The more stressed we are, the more difficult it is to face our feelings and the greater hold our addictions have on us. Studies on rats trained to self-administer drugs have shown that the more stress the rat is under, the more likely it is to rely on the substance to cope.[5]

Finally, we keep on doing what we've always done because that's what we're used to – it's the path of least resistance. We are creatures of habit, and if we've spent 30 years using coffee as our tool for waking up in the morning, letting go of our caffeine fix is going to take effort – it means retraining ourselves to behave in a new way.

This is especially hard if we are using substances (whether narcotics or nicotine) that send our brain and body systems into withdrawal when we stop. It is also difficult to stop if our addictions are socially approved of – why should we cut down on shopping, drinking or rushing around, if that's what everyone around us is doing? The more our addictive behaviours are reinforced, by ourselves and by others, the harder it becomes to go against the grain and give them up.

But it's worth going against the grain. Why? Because facing our feelings brings rewards that are greater and longer-lasting than those offered by our addictions. It's true that when we stop acting compulsively, we open ourselves up to painful emotions – we may start to feel the sadness or fear that we have previously been trying to shy away from. But at the same time, we open ourselves up to the vividness of life, including feelings of joy, love, peace, connection – that also get suppressed when we run away from our pain. By creating space where our addictive patterns used to be, we free up the whole of our emotional register. Instead of the deadness of addiction, we start to feel more present to the whole of our experience – the pain *and* the joy.

FEELINGS, ADDICTION AND THE BRAIN

When we practise meditation, we are starting to act counter to patterns that we, and the generations before us, have been repeating for a very long time. These patterns are deeply woven into us, so much so that they have become 'hardwired' into our brain. There is, therefore, real effort required to come off autopilot and make new choices. Perhaps this is why Tibetan Buddhist teacher Chögyam Trungpa Rinpoche has called this, not mindfulness of feelings, but 'mindfulness of effort'. By making the effort to practise mindfulness – the effort of letting go – we may be able to rewire ourselves *away* from addiction.

The part of our brains that regulates emotions is called the *limbic system*. The limbic system is quite primitive – it evolved before other, more 'advanced' parts of the brain such as the prefrontal cortex, which is associated with qualities such as reflection and self-awareness. The prefrontal cortex is relatively larger in humans than in other animals – it is a mark of our sophistication.

When we are under stress, however, it's the limbic system that kicks in – it takes less than a quarter of a second to trigger feelings of fear or anger in us, provoking our kneejerk 'fight or flight' response. In the face of stress we tend to react like animals, instinctively – we lash out, or run away. Unfortunately, the more we face stress and react impulsively, the more sensitive the limbic system gets – the neurons in this, like any other part of the brain, get strengthened with use. On a physiological level, this may be how our habitual patterns get reinforced.

Meanwhile, the parts of the prefrontal cortex involved in making choices tend to get bypassed when we are stressed – making us even more likely to act in an unreflective way.

When we practise mindfulness, we are taking a more evolved approach – deliberately choosing to employ the prefrontal cortex to decide whether to listen to what our limbic system is urging us to do.

That doesn't mean we won't still experience fear and anger when we practise mindfulness – the limbic system will still generate powerful urges and feelings. But we might not be so prone to getting caught in instinctive reactions when they aren't helpful. Rather than breeding more fear, or more anger, we instead cultivate awareness, resilience and wise decision-making.

There is support for this from Dr Sara Lazar's studies, which we mentioned in Chapter 2. She found that a key part of the limbic system – the amygdala, which is sometimes called the brain's fear centre – became smaller in the brains of people who practised mindfulness meditation. Studies have also demonstrated that in stressed animals, the amygdala tends to grow.[6]

David Creswell and colleagues at UCLA have also found that people who are more naturally mindful have less active amygdalas, and show more activity in parts of the prefrontal cortex.[7] Being mindful, it seems, could be a way of turning down the reactivity of the limbic system – enabling us to deal with emotion-provoking situations in a more considered, reflective manner.

The ability to train our brains and bodies to respond differently to fear could be especially relevant for addiction treatment. When we do anything that makes us feel good, we activate the brain's 'reward circuit'. The reward circuit releases dopamine, a neurotransmitter that creates immediate feelings of pleasure. Parts of the brain – such as the amygdala – then remember what gave us this pleasure, and trigger urges and cravings to do it again. Unfortunately, this means that when we do something that makes us feel better in the short term, we'll still feel impelled to repeat it, even when we know intellectually that it has negative long-term consequences.

This is how people get addicted to drugs such as cocaine, which flood the brain with dopamine. The user might feel good for a while, but there is also a comedown – the brain starts to make less of its own dopamine, or cuts down on dopamine receptors to try and maintain its chemical balance, so that without the drug, the users may feel depressed or anxious. If they keep using, they'll need more and more to get the same high, while withdrawal leaves them more and more unhappy, leading to further cravings. Former drug users will keep getting cravings for a very long time after they've stopped, because the brain has been changed – it is conditioned to expect the drug. Other pleasure-seeking activities – such as eating and sex – can have a similar effect (although over a longer time period) if we rely on them too much.

To free ourselves of addictive patterns, we have to find alternative ways to respond to the feelings, urges and cravings that our limbic system generates. Mindfulness is one way – by using our awareness to watch, stay with and respond differently to addictive urges and difficult emotions, we are weakening the drive to react impulsively, and training our ability to choose new behaviours. We may still experience strong feelings – urges and cravings to act in ways that are harmful – but the more we practise, the less likely we are to succumb to them. We can begin to rewire our brains away from addiction.

Chögyam Trungpa Rinpoche said that when we try to protect ourselves from our feelings, we are creating a cocoon for ourselves, covering ourselves with layers of thick psychic armour.[8] In this cocoon, we feel safe – well defended from the dangers of the world. But the cocoon also shuts out the light of life – we might feel less vulnerable inside our shell, but we also feel claustrophobic, dark, stuffy and restricted.

EMERGING FROM OUR COCOON

Coming out of the cocoon doesn't mean acting out all our feelings. When we rage at someone, we might think we're very connected to our emotions, but we're wrong. Instead, by screaming at everyone around us we are trying to get rid of feelings as fast as we can. This too is self-defeating

– by dumping our emotions on other people, we create more misery for ourselves. People shout back or avoid our company, and we are left with even more painful feelings to contend with, perhaps embarrassment and loneliness on top of our initial anger. Acting out our feelings isn't really experiencing them – it's just another form of avoidance.

Mindfulness practice shows us how to *relate* with our feelings in a different way. We notice them, stay with them and watch them pass through us. When we practise mindfulness of our feelings, we are applying the same methods that we used to work with our breath, our body and our thoughts – we directly experience our feelings with curiosity and without judgement. By taking the time to be with our emotions, gently, kindly, without attachment or avoidance, we start to gain a direct, deeper understanding of how they operate. From this understanding we can start to respond more wisely to them.

Because we are opening ourselves up to more of our experience, our lives start to become richer. We become more sensitised not just to pain but to the everyday magic of our existence – the majesty of the sun at daybreak, the touch of a lover's skin, the beating of our own heart. Only by letting go of our addictions – at least to some extent – can we really make contact with the wonder of our lives.

NOTICING FEELINGS

We can start, as usual, with the breath. Taking an in-breath, start to bring your awareness into your body. Allow your mind to follow the breath – through your nostrils,

165

down the back of your throat, into your lungs. As you exhale, repeat the process, noticing the sensation as you release the air from your lungs and it moves out, over your tongue, between your lips and back into the air – exchanging precious oxygen for waste carbon dioxide from every cell in your body.

Now, with each inhalation, imagine that the air you breathe is warming you up, bringing you alive, nourishing you, allowing you to feel – not just your body sensations, but your emotions as well. Notice, as the air flows in and out, how these emotions feel: Are you feeling joy, anger, sadness or fear? Can you investigate their texture? What does anger feel like to you? Do you feel hot – like your blood is boiling, or that there's a fist punching out from inside your face? Whereabouts in your body are you feeling your emotions? Is there happiness in your heart, fear in your stomach, sadness in your chest, anxiety in your legs? How are these feelings expressed in your body? Like a wave, a gust of wind, a heavy stone or a bouncing rabbit?

Can you feel more than one feeling at once? Can sadness be there at the same time as joy? How do the two connect and interact with one another? Maybe you're not feeling any particular emotion at the moment – perhaps you're feeling flat, a kind of nothingness – in which case, just notice that. Remember that we aren't trying to create any particular experience here – we are simply becoming aware of what is there, seeing it without manipulation.

When you are mindful of your emotions, you don't have to suppress them, but neither do you have to identify with them. With this practice, we are placing our feelings in context, giving them their natural place in our body, experiencing them with our minds. When experiencing a pleasant feeling, we simply know that we are experiencing a pleasant feeling, and when experiencing a painful feeling, we know that, too.

GIVING YOUR EMOTIONS SPACE

Mindfulness practice is a direct antidote to the forces that keep our addictions in place. By paying attention to our feelings, we attain greater awareness of them. We start to experience them more, and we see how they affect us. Instead of reaching immediately for a cigarette, a drink, an explanation, a walnut whip or our wallets, we let go of clinging and actually look at what we've been trying to avoid.

When we notice our feelings mindfully, we are also training ourselves in staying with them. We are learning that it is possible to tolerate difficult emotions. Remember from the last chapter what Dixon said about paying attention to pain: 'Surprisingly often, you realise it isn't as dreadful as you thought'? Could the same be true of our feelings? Is our anger really so intolerable that we have to dump it on other people? Is our worry so overwhelming that we have to reach for a cigarette? Is our sadness so unbearable that we have to cover it over with rationalisation? Often it feels like it, but when we stay with our feelings in mindfulness meditation, we sometimes make a surprising discovery: we *can* bear our emotional pain without running from it.

By staying mindfully with our feelings, we are starting to let go of our habitual reactions to them. By creating a gap in which we can be with our emotions rather than impulsively trying to get rid of them, we give ourselves the chance to contemplate what to do next – we naturally give ourselves a greater freedom of choice over how to respond. Do we want to do what we've always done, to follow our habitual patterns, or do we want to make a change, to choose a new behaviour? Practising mindfulness, we give ourselves more power to make an informed choice.

We may even find that we don't have to *do anything* – discovering instead that feelings naturally pass through and dissolve without our help, just like thoughts. Sometimes all we need to do is give emotions space in our bodies, allowing their energy to arise, exist and leave us naturally. This is, after all, what the word 'emotion' implies – a process of outward movement. Letting emotions dissolve naturally in this way is what Tibetan Buddhists call 'self-liberation'.

PRACTICE: Mindfulness of Feelings – Riding the Waves of Emotion

The experience of strong emotions can often feel like a wave, crashing through our minds and bodies. Their power can seem awesome, but, like waves, emotions arise, peak and fall, and they can be surfed. By riding the emotion – being with it – it may well dissolve faster than if we give it more energy by ruminating about it, acting it out or trying to suppress it through addictive behaviour.

This exercise can help you learn how to ride the waves of feeling. You can try it for a while when you are practising mindfulness of breathing. Then, once you've developed your surfing skills, you can use it at any time strong feelings, urges or cravings arise.

STEP ONE
As you feel the emotion, urge or craving arise, first notice how it is being expressed in your body. Does it feel hot or cold? Is it in your chest, your stomach or your head? Is it pulsing, rising up fast through you or is it moving more slowly? How strong is the feeling – just a little ripple, or a giant, seemingly irresistible wave?

STEP TWO
If you find it helpful, you can label the feeling as you might do a thought. Rather than saying to yourself 'mind wandering' or 'thinking', you could say 'anger' or 'sadness' or 'fear'. Is there a mental storyline attached to the emotion ('Why does she always leave her cup in the sink and not put it in the dishwasher?', 'My neighbour is such a noisy bastard, doesn't he ever think about anyone else's feelings?', 'I can't face another day in that office, I just want to go and curl up under the duvet', 'God, I need a drink!')? If there is, just acknowledge it and let it go like any other thought. Continue to rest your attention on the emotion.

STEP THREE
Having taken the measure of the emotion, place your awareness on it, as you would the breath. Your awareness is the surfboard you can use to ride the emotion. Rather than fighting the feeling, suppressing it or acting it out, see if you can just stay with it as it moves through your body. Be kind to the feeling, even if the feeling itself feels unkind.

STEP FOUR

Notice how the feeling changes over time. Does it become stronger, or less tangible? Does its location in your body change? Is it starting to turn into another emotion? How is the feeling different after you have stayed with it for 1 minute, 2 minutes, 5 minutes, 10 minutes or longer? Do the thoughts that come with the emotion also change? How is it not to act on the feeling, but just to carry on watching it? Do you want to jump up and do something – phone a friend, eat something, go to work, rearrange your bedroom? What's your habitual response to feeling like you're feeling now, and what is it like simply to stay with your experience in mindfulness meditation?

STEP FIVE

Stay with the wave of emotion as it follows its cycle – see how it naturally swells up, reaches a crest and then rolls out of the body? Perhaps there are several waves going on in your body all at once – can you rest your awareness on more than one feeling, more than one wave at a time?

STEP SIX

Whatever you do next, see if you can maintain some awareness of the feeling you have been riding. Check in with it at regular intervals – where in the body is it now? How has it changed since you were first aware of it? Has it been superseded by another feeling? And how is this emotion influencing how you behave – is it doing so in a way that's useful, or harmful? If the latter, can you hold the feeling in your awareness without letting it take you over?

There are times when it is appropriate to act, when our feelings are telling us we need to do something. But once we have started to bring ourselves into balance with mindfulness, we can act more appropriately. Instead of being dominated by our emotional life (or our attempts to avoid it) we can take our feelings into account, reflect on them and respond to them in a more measured, intelligent way.

IN TWO MINDS

There's a neat way of describing this which is sometimes used in Dialectical Behaviour Therapy (DBT), a mindfulness-based treatment that has been shown to be helpful for people with borderline personality disorder. People with borderline personality disorder are often *overly* identified with their feelings – they can find it hard to contain their emotions and, when these are painful, they are easily triggered into acting out self-harming, addictive behaviours as an expression of their pain.

DBT teaches us that we have two minds – an emotional mind and a rational mind. If we live in thrall to our emotional mind, acting primarily on the basis of our feelings, we will find ourselves too easily tossed around by our anger, our fear or our sadness – like people with borderline personality disorder, we will find it difficult to contain ourselves, and we'll tend to act impulsively and irrationally. On the other hand, if we are dominated by our rational mind, our experience will be limited – we will always be thinking about our life and never really experiencing it.

When we pay attention mindfully, we are using both our 'emotional mind' and our 'rational mind'. We don't cover our feelings with addictive behaviours, but neither do we impulsively act them out. We start to be able to integrate our emotions and our intellect, giving us new scope to respond to their messages in a more balanced way. In DBT, this integration of the emotional and rational mind is called 'wise mind'.

Trials of DBT among women with borderline personality disorder have shown it can lead to less self-harming, less drug abuse, fewer suicide attempts and fewer hospitalisations.[9] DBT has also been proven to reduce distress and anger levels, help people adjust better socially and improve their overall mental health. On the basis of this evidence, DBT is now recommended for use in the NHS by the National Institute for Health and Clinical Excellence – a second major official endorsement for mindfulness-based approaches.

Dialectical Behaviour Therapy is just one of several new treatments that use mindfulness to show people how to deal more wisely with their feelings. Professor Alan Marlatt is Director of the Addictive Behaviours Research Center at the University of Washington – he has been working to develop treatments for people with alcohol problems for almost 40 years. His first brush with the benefits of meditation was a personal one – he was encouraged to try it by his doctor when diagnosed with high blood pressure early in his career.

Finding it helpful, Marlatt read up on some of the early research which showed meditation could induce a 'relaxation response', and he thought it might also work for some of his addiction patients. This hunch was backed up by some of his own early research, which found that meditation was as effective as exercise in reducing drinkers' alcohol consumption, and more effective than deep muscle relaxation and daily periods of quiet reading.[10]

Marlatt has since pioneered the use of cognitive behavioural therapy (CBT) to help prevent relapse among alcohol and drug users. The key element of relapse prevention is encouraging the development of coping skills to be used when stressful situations occur. Giving up their substance of choice is just the first step in recovery for alcoholics and addicts – the next challenge is learning how to manage the difficult feelings that stress creates, without resorting to the old reaction of taking a drink or drug. Marlatt recommends mindfulness as a way of coping with addictive urges – a 'being' skill that can be cultivated as an alternative to the impulsive, destructive acting out of the addictive behaviour.

Inspired by Jon Kabat-Zinn and the developers of mindfulness-based cognitive therapy, Professor Marlatt and his team have created a course to help people with alcohol problems. Mindfulness-Based Relapse Prevention (MBRP) teaches meditation as a way of tolerating the inevitable urges that impel people to act on their addictions. By cultivating their ability to pay attention to and stay in the present moment – even when it contains difficult feelings – MBRP trains them to interrupt the addictive habit, watching and accepting cravings rather than being driven by them. Learning how not to act on addictive urges builds confidence that they can be withstood. Over time, as drug and alcohol use fades into the past, the cravings themselves may begin to dissipate.

At the same time as Professor Marlatt was developing his course in Washington, London-based psychiatrist Dr Paramabandhu Groves had a similar idea. He had already begun teaching mindfulness-based cognitive therapy to patients with depression, and quickly realised that virtually the same course could be taught to people who were struggling to stop abusing alcohol or drugs. Dr Groves describes mindfulness as an ABC skill, because it fosters awareness (A), the ability to 'be with' feelings (B), and the capacity to make new, wiser choices (C) – all tools which recovering addicts need to stop them being drawn back into their compulsive substance use.

Dr Groves now runs Mindfulness-Based Relapse Prevention (MBRP) courses both as part of his day job with the Camden and Islington Mental Health and Social Care Trust, and at Breathing Space, a social enterprise which offers mindfulness-based services to people in the East End of London.

CARLA'S EXPERIENCE

Carla, 40, took a mindfulness-based relapse-prevention course six months after giving up alcohol. Without it, she suspects she may not have made it into long-term sobriety.

After a 20-year-relationship came to an end, Carla's alcohol consumption sky-rocketed. 'I basically lost myself in alcohol,' she remembers, 'self-medicating to deal with the emotions.'

Eventually, she was accepted into a detox programme, but, as with most substance users, she was plagued by negative thoughts and powerful emotions. 'I really struggled with stress and cravings, and especially my thinking processes,' she says. About six months into her treatment, the participants in her recovery programme were invited for an open day at Breathing Space, and Carla went along with her key worker. 'I had a chat with one of the people there, and he recommended the mindfulness-based relapse-prevention course. He said it might help me deal with my thoughts, and some of my overwhelming feelings.'

She was open to trying meditation – her mum used to practise it when she was growing up and had said it was helpful. Carla says she 'doesn't deal well with stress', and has been prone to panic attacks. She was also signed off work for a while with anxiety. Because of her anxiety, the mindfulness programme was not an easy ride at first. 'Initially, I found it quite hard being around people I didn't know. But we all had something in common, so that made me feel safe.' As the course progressed, she started to relax.

The weeks passed, and Carla began to notice some 'dramatic' changes. 'I was able to focus on things more, and I became a lot more confident – more comfortable in my skin. I started to accept myself.' Learning how to practise working with thoughts and feelings in a mindful way was especially useful for her. 'The meditation helped me allow things to pass rather than thinking about them too much. Before, my mind was constantly working – I couldn't shut it off, which is typical of people suffering an addiction. I used to have problems sleeping, but now I'm able to go to sleep quite easily.'

Mindfulness also helped her cope better with her urges to drink. 'It helps with being able to sit with cravings,' she explains. 'I can stay with the feeling rather than avoiding it. Ultimately, the craving moves into another feeling.'

Two and a half years later, Carla continues to use the techniques she learned on the course. 'If my mind starts to race, or if I am over-analysing and thinking too much, I can bring myself into the moment and focus on what I'm doing. When I have a panicky feeling I can calm myself down and relax with the breathing – bringing myself back into my body, asking how the ground feels under my feet or what emotion I'm having, rather than my mind wandering off in a negative way. You can do it when you're brushing your teeth, having a shower, or on the Tube.'

Carla's life is now back on track, but she says that, without mindfulness, 'I almost think I'd be drinking again.' She's now training to be an alcohol and drug worker, and frequently recommends the MBRP course to others. 'Whenever I come across somebody who's really struggling with anxiety, craving and negative thinking, I recommend mindfulness to them. It has helped me focus on what I want, and I can now be comfortable and real with myself. Mindfulness feels like something special that's a part of me.'

FIGHTING ADDICTION

Mindfulness-based relapse-prevention is still in its early days – the programme's effectiveness is now being researched – but the early evidence is encouraging.[10] There are lots of similarities between the struggles of people with chronic physical illness, mental health problems and addictions – most of them have to deal with stress, negative thinking and painful body sensations or feelings – and there is, therefore, every reason to suspect that the mindfulness practices that so clearly help the first two groups might also benefit the third. A study conducted by the University of Washington team to evaluate the impact of another mindfulness intervention – an intensive 10-day course offered to inmates recently released from prison – has also offered encouragement.[12] It found that, three months after the course, those who had taken part took far fewer drugs and drank far less alcohol than a control group who didn't.

Mindfulness courses have also been tried as a way of supporting people to give up cigarettes. James Davis and his colleagues at the University of Wisconsin offered a mindfulness-based stress-reduction course to a group of smokers.[13] When they experienced withdrawal symptoms such as irritability, sore throats or headaches, participants were encouraged simply to notice these mindfully, just as they would any other body sensations, thoughts or feelings – in a non-judgemental, friendly and interested way. Although the participants were given a smoking quit date, they were encouraged not to focus too much on the 'goal' of stopping – instead, the course was designed primarily to help them cultivate a more mindful approach to living.

Of the 18 participants, 5 dropped out before the day came to quit. But of the remaining 13, only 3 had relapsed 6 weeks after the course – a 56 per cent success rate (or almost 80 per cent if you exclude those who didn't complete the programme). This compares to a previous group who were given just counselling and in which only 33 per cent were still non-smokers after 6 weeks. It was a small study, but nevertheless indicates the potential for mindfulness to help people quit – either alone or alongside some of the

more conventional medical approaches which have also
proven effective.

Mindfulness is also being used to help treat eating
disorders. Jean Kristeller, Professor of Psychology at Indiana
State University, together with her colleague Brendan
Hallett has developed a programme called Mindfulness-
based Eating Awareness Training (MB-EAT). Just as people
who are addicted to drink or drugs get cravings for their
preferred substance, so people whose 'drug of choice' is
food have a tendency to cope with stress by overeating,
often bingeing on foods high in sugar or carbohydrates.
Eating disorders are especially difficult addictions to
handle, because, unlike drugs or alcohol, it isn't possible to
steer clear of temptation – we all need to eat, several times
a day. People who are drawn to binge have to find a way to
face their triggers without succumbing to habitual patterns.

As well as mindfulness of breathing, body and feelings,
Mindfulness-Based Eating Awareness Training incorporates
several meditation practices designed to help participants
develop a new kind of relationship with food.

This is actually not a new development – in mindfulness-
based stress-reduction and mindfulness-based cognitive
therapy courses, the very first exercise consists of asking
people to eat a raisin mindfully – to hold it in their hand
first and investigate its texture as if they have never seen
one before, and then to place it slowly into their mouth,
roll it around with their tongue, taste its flavour and chew it
with full awareness. Only after several minutes of mindful
investigation is the raisin finally swallowed.

Participants in MBSR and MBCT are also given homework where they practise eating one meal a week in this way – rather than wolfing down food quickly or greedily, the emphasis is on being fully present to the experience of eating. By developing a more mindful relationship with food, we can learn to enjoy eating, not as an addictive escape but as a present-moment experience – savouring food in our mouth and body rather than stuffing it into us as a way of calming down.

In MB-EAT, mindful eating takes centre stage. By learning how to be mindful of their bodies, participants can start to answer questions such as: 'Am I really hungry? Do I want to eat because my body needs it, or because I'm trying to distract myself from some other sensation or emotion?' and 'At what point is my body full? Am I carrying on eating even when my body has had enough?' By learning to be mindful of thoughts and feelings, participants become aware of the mental and emotional triggers that can spark a binge, and experience how those triggers naturally pass through their awareness, arising, changing and dissolving without any need to act on them. Through the raisin exercise, and through mindful meals, they learn to appreciate eating food as a fundamentally wholesome part of being alive, rather than as an addictive activity.

And it seems to work. In a trial carried out by Kristeller and Hallett, an MB-EAT course was given to 18 women with a diagnosis of binge-eating disorder – on average, they weighed 17 stone, and went on food binges more than four times a week.[14] But by the end of the course, the average number of weekly binges had dropped to between one and two, while only four of the participants continued to show symptoms severe enough to be classed as binge-eating disorder. The women also reported feeling less depressed and anxious.

For many of us, eating is one of our most dangerous habits – with a quarter of us now classified as obese, dysfunctional eating patterns kill far more of us than less socially acceptable addictions to drugs like heroin or crack cocaine. We eat not just when we are hungry, but when we are angry, lonely, tired or bored, filling ourselves up with calories that our bodies don't really need. Diabetes, high blood pressure, heart disease, arthritis and some types of cancer can all be brought on by eating too much of the wrong kinds of food.

Some of us might not think of ourselves as having an eating disorder, but most people can relate to the same dysfunctional patterns of eating that characterise conditions like anorexia and bulimia – we pig out because we've had a bad day at work, or we've had an argument, and then we feel guilty because we're worried about gaining weight. Consumed by shame, we may then punish ourselves with a stringent diet, which lasts until we have another bad day or another set of difficult feelings – at which point the cycle begins again.

Even when we're not bingeing or dieting, our eating habits tend to be mindless. Rather than paying attention to what our body needs, we fill it with junk. Rather than savouring the smell, taste and texture of what we put into our mouths, we shovel it in, perhaps simultaneously listening to the news, watching a programme on TV, replying to emails during an 'al desko' office lunch, or even just reading the cereal packet while we have our breakfast. When we eat like this, we are dishonouring our body, our mind *and* our feelings. We are out of touch with our body and ignoring the signals it sends us about hunger and being full, carried away by habitual thought patterns that tell us to eat the same foods in the same way we have always done. And we are unconsciously reacting to feelings – perhaps loneliness, frustration, grief – in a way that separates us from them and perpetuates our emotional disconnection from ourselves, others and our world, as well as hampering our ability to respond to them more creatively.

We can all benefit from the practice of mindful eating – a middle way between the extremes of binge and diet. When we eat mindfully, we pay attention to how our body is before, during and after our meal. We become aware of our thoughts and all the messages they contain about diet (some may be positive –'Mmm, I'm enjoying this chocolate bar much more than if I were rushing it,' and many may be negative 'My mother always said I was a fat cow! I'm so self-indulgent') and we watch them all with a kindly awareness rather than criticism. We notice our feelings as we change our usual pattern of eating – does taking our meal slowly release feelings of anxiety or anger, or do we feel joyful at taking this time to really delve into the sensual pleasure of food? And, of course, we really pay attention to the food itself, appreciating one of the exquisitely wonderful and fundamental experiences of being alive.

PRACTICE: Mindful Eating

You can practise mindful eating with any meal, but why not start with something simple and short, like eating an orange? Find somewhere quiet to sit and begin by simply picking up the orange and moving it around in your hands. Notice its weight, feel its shape – is it very round or slightly misshapen? Is it hard, or a little soft in places? Really look at the orange – notice its bright, vibrant, natural colour. Feel its texture – examine the tiny dimples in its skin, and any roughness or wrinkles on its surface.

Now spend a moment imagining where the orange has come from, the tree it grew on, the earth that provided the water and nutrients it needed, the sunshine that ripened it. Think about how long it took to grow, the farmer who picked it and the journey it has taken – perhaps using many different modes of transport, under the care of many different people. Isn't it remarkable how it has got into your hands now?

Start to peel the orange. Notice how the zest gets under your nails, the smell of the citrus that is released as you tear into the skin. Pay attention as you gradually reveal the flesh of the fruit inside.

Now separate out one segment from the orange. Notice the sensation as any juice runs over your fingers – feel the sticky sugariness as it dries on your hands. Place the segment in your mouth but don't chew it – just hold it on your tongue and move it around in your mouth for a minute or so. Now, bite into it! Taste the burst of flavour that's released – is it all sweet or a little bit sour? Chew it slowly, much slower than you usually would – and pay attention to the texture of the flesh of the orange, the juice dripping over your tongue. Savour the flavour.

When you're ready to swallow the segment, move it carefully to the back of your tongue and towards your epiglottis. As you take a gulp of saliva to draw the segment down, feel the muscles in the back of your throat squeeze it into your oesophagus. What sensations are there as the piece of orange slips down into your body?

Continue eating each segment of the orange in this same way – one piece at a time. Notice the change in intensity of the experience as you keep eating. Perhaps you'll find you aren't enjoying the taste so much with later segments. Perhaps pause halfway through the orange and ask yourself, 'Do I really want the rest of it?' When you feel satisfied, stop eating and put any left away for later. If you haven't eaten the whole orange, how does it feel to leave some of it for another time? Are there any thoughts associated with eating only part of a piece of fruit?

You don't have to munch everything at a snail's pace to eat mindfully – but if you're not used to paying much attention to your food, it can be helpful to go slowly in this exaggerated way. Mindful eating isn't so much about the speed we eat at as our ability to stay in contact with our experience – body, mind and feelings – while we are eating. But it is like any other skill that we learn: we can only do it at speed once we've had some practice. Perhaps you could aim to eat one meal a week in this way, or just the first few mouthfuls of each meal. See if you can pay particular attention to the sensations of hunger and fullness in your stomach – so many of us keep eating long after our bodies have had enough. With mindfulness, we can really feel how much food we want and need.

ERIC'S EXPERIENCE

Eric, 28, is a successful businessman, and now weighs about 15 stone. But it wasn't always like that. He has a history of intense anxiety, and his means of escape from it was food – lots of it. At one point, his overeating resulted in him tipping the scales at more than twice his current weight.

'Obesity was just an expression of my anxiety,' explains Eric. 'It was debilitating, and food had a sedating effect. It seemed to bring me down, in a good way – it made the anxiety manageable. After a long day at work I would come in the door and I had to eat sugary, starchy stuff to reach that point of calm. It was only specific foods that would do it – if I had protein, like a steak with broccoli or something, I never felt that feeling I was looking for to calm me down. It was like a kind of sedation – an anaesthetic.'

Eric's anxiety dates back to his childhood. 'I didn't sleep from the time I can remember till the time I left home. I used to have nightmares of being kidnapped – I was constantly frightened.' Eating offered solace, but at a price. 'There was one pivotal moment … I was 17, walking up the stairs at school. It was only two flights, but when I got to the top my heart was racing – I weighed just over 30 stone at that point. I remember looking over the top of the stairs and thinking, "If you're going to live, then something has to change." When you're eating as much as I was, you're essentially destroying your body.'

Eric made a decision to lose weight – but his struggles weren't over. He tried both exercise and dieting, but nothing much changed. 'The way Western medicine focuses on obesity, it's all about eating less food and burning calories. That's certainly a component but it didn't really deal with the main issue. For me, learning what foods are healthy and all the behaviour modification and exercise were all secondary, because I was still being plagued by anxiety, and that was what led me to eat in the first place. Dealing with that was the crucial part.'

But Eric couldn't deal with his anxiety while he still didn't understand how it operated, and why it led him to eat. 'The self-destruction was so subconscious that I didn't even notice what was happening,' he says. 'When I was shovelling food in my mouth I didn't really know what I was doing or why – I was eating before I even knew that I wanted to eat!'

Eventually, Eric was given a mindfulness-based stress-reduction CD by a friend's mother. Finally, things started to change. By practising mindfulness Eric feels he has grown 'a consciousness that didn't exist before, a sense of clarity'. This enabled him to notice what his 'addiction' to food was doing to him. By practising, he was able to open up a gap between whatever thought, emotion or sensation triggered his compulsion to eat and the act of bingeing. He has been able to let go of his automatic, habitual reaction to fear and anxiety.

'Now eating comes as a result of making a decision, versus feeding a need,' he says. 'Before, there wasn't even an option. It was almost like taking in air – I felt like I needed to eat immediately or I wouldn't survive. It doesn't seem to be that way any more. Now eating is no longer just a reaction – I consciously consider everything that I put into my mouth. I get the urge, yes, but I don't act on it any more. I am able to manage the anxiety.'

There seems no reason why the same mechanisms that seem to work in mindfulness-based stress reduction and mindfulness-based cognitive therapy should not apply to people with addictions, with all the same benefits. But once again, the scope for mindfulness could well go way beyond those who are desperate enough to reach health services. At its root, much of the overconsumption and much of the stress in our speedy, overactive world is due to addictive tendencies. By doing less, and noticing more, we are starting to reverse that pattern – with mindfulness we can engage with our feelings, accepting them and relating with them directly, in the moment.

Mindfulness-based relapse prevention may be new, but the use of mindfulness to deal with addiction isn't – it was a fundamental part of the Buddha's prescription for letting go of the clinging and craving that causes human suffering. It doesn't matter whether our clinging is to heroin, the internet, money, sex, cigarettes, relationships, ice cream or success, when we use anything as a way of avoiding the experience of the moment, rather than engaging with it, we are setting ourselves up for suffering.

Using mindfulness to practise working skilfully with our feelings is therefore a crucial part of the mindful manifesto – if we can learn how to be more aware of our emotions, without reacting to them impulsively, we start to loosen the grip of addiction that has such a hold in our world. It may not always be easy to relate to our feelings directly, but when we do, we free ourselves up to experience everything as a miracle. Surely that makes it worthwhile?

MINDFULNESS OF FEELINGS: SUGGESTIONS FOR PRACTICE

BEING GENTLE
When we stay with our feelings in mindfulness, we are embedding new patterns, and this takes time – indeed, it is

a life-long process of becoming gradually more skilled in our practice. If you succumb to a craving, urge or feeling, it isn't a failure – just another opportunity to come back to the present moment. You can notice the effect that acting out old patterns has, and compare it to what happens when you are able to be mindful. But don't be hard on yourself – we all have the tendency to fall back on what we know when things get tough. Being mindful means letting go of harsh judgement as well as unhelpful behaviours.

DEALING WITH INCREASED SENSITIVITY

Just as some people report *more* thoughts when they start practising meditation, so others report that their feelings get more intense. This isn't because meditation is making them worse, it's because they are beginning to drop their defences. If your feelings appear to gather in strength when you practise, this may mean you are starting to become more alive. Remember that this will also allow you to experience more fully and enjoy pleasant feelings when they come along.

STRETCHING THE COMFORT ZONE

We can try extending our ability to stay with feelings. When you practise mindfulness of breathing, see if you can increase your practice time a bit further – perhaps adding another 5 or 10 minutes once a week. Notice the emotions that come up during this extra sitting time: can you practise surfing the waves of these feelings?

USING DISTRACTIONS

Another way to develop our capacity to stay with feelings is to use whatever natural distractions arise when we practise.

Can you resist the urge to scratch an itch, move your aching leg, roll your shoulders or get up and make a cup of tea? It doesn't have to become a torture session – just play with it and see if you can stay still a little longer than you usually would. Each time we do this, we are letting go of our compulsive tendency to 'do' and strengthening our ability to 'be'.

NOT BEING ATTACHED TO 'HAPPINESS'

Sometimes when we practise we may experience strong feelings of joy, contentment, peace or love. If you experience feelings like this, that's great, but beware of getting too attached to them – otherwise we risk disappointment and frustration when they change. Real happiness comes not from holding on to positive feelings, but from being able to be fundamentally at peace whether our emotions are pleasant or unpleasant.

Jonty's Experience

I do a lot of work in the field of drug misuse, usually working with patients who have addictions to hard drugs such as crack cocaine or heroin, but actually almost every consultation I participate in has change at its heart. As we have come to understand more and more about the causes of illnesses there is an ever-greater responsibility on all of us to take care of our health. We need to avoid those things that contribute to disease, such as smoking, and do more to help prevent ill-health by, for example, taking regular exercise and eating healthily. But these changes are notoriously difficult to make. There cannot be many of my patients, if any, who have not heard or read about the risks associated with being overweight. And almost everyone I know who is overweight recognises it as being something they need and want to change … They also know what they need to do to lose weight – yet somehow it is not as simple as that – putting the theory into practice is really hard.

I cannot count the number of times I have tried to get into a regular routine of taking some exercise, eating more healthily, not snacking on the biscuits we keep in reception, or switching off the TV and picking up a book in the evening when I get home. But my unhealthy habits are so automatic and so comforting that, before I know it, I am back to square one. What mindfulness does is provide a very useful, practical bridge across this gap of ambivalence; it helps us remember our new intentions, without guilt or criticism, and motivates us to change because we want to, not because we should. I do now do some of those things I have mentioned (at least some of the time!) but I do them because I want to take care of my body and my mind. I've started to notice how I feel when I don't eat healthily or take regular exercise, how it affects my stress levels and my concentration. Mindfulness allows us to notice what we are doing to ourselves, how it really makes us feel, and then allows us to break our unhealthy habits by disengaging our autopilot for long enough to make different choices – based on caring for ourselves and not driven by guilt or insecurity.

Ed's Experience

Giving up smoking was one of the best things I've ever done for myself – and mindfulness was definitely a key factor. Having picked up the habit in my early teens, by my early thirties I was thoroughly sick of the smell, the cost, the coughing and the likely damage to my health. I'd tried giving up before, but it never lasted – I wasn't able to stay with the discomfort of withdrawal long enough for the new habit of non-smoking to take root. After a few years of meditation, however, I was ready to try again. It still wasn't easy – but this time I not only really had the desire, but I'd also developed, somewhat, the practice of staying with experience, even when it was uncomfortable. In the early days, each time I felt the craving to puff, I'd breathe in, place my attention on the feeling of desire, and ride it through – staying in the moment rather than acting on the feeling it brought. Before long, the desire to smoke would subside, and I could congratulate myself for further embedding my new choice not to light up. As the weeks passed the waves began to subside, and after a couple of months I was able to sit in a pub and have a drink while people smoked around me (this was before the smoking ban) – something I once thought I'd never manage. Now, some four years later, I hardly ever feel any pangs for nicotine. I do still have plenty of addictive tendencies – all too easily I can find myself eating, drinking, working, rushing or even reading books as a way of avoiding life, shutting myself off from painful contact with experience. But I always have a choice – a glass of wine can either be an escape or a fully enjoyed pleasure, depending on whether I can remember to engage with it mindfully or not. Can I sip slowly, savour the taste and appreciate the intoxication without overindulging? Not always – but a great deal more often than before I started practising. Fortunately, mindfulness has also taught me to give up striving for perfection!

CHAPTER SIX

MINDFULNESS OF LIFE

Open your eyes and extend your awareness to take in the world around you – bring mindfulness into your daily life and become more skilful in your approach to any situation that arises.

Meditation is sometimes criticised for being a selfish pursuit. 'If you want to be kind and compassionate, why aren't you out helping the homeless, rather than sitting at home doing nothing? How can watching your thoughts and feelings make the world a better place – it's just navel-gazing, isn't it?'

It's a good question – the first three foundations of mindfulness *are* focused on learning how to relate more effectively with our internal experience. But there is good reason for this: unless we first generate some awareness of and ability to handle our habitual patterns by focusing in on them, we run the risk of continuing to act them out, perhaps unconsciously. We may keep doing harm, to ourselves and others, even when our intentions are good. Chögyam Trungpa Rinpoche memorably termed this tendency 'idiot compassion' – we think we're helping when we're actually making things worse. We can't take our mindfulness out into the world until we have gained some understanding of what it tells us about ourselves. It's a bit like the advice we're given in aeroplane safety demonstrations – in an emergency, put your own oxygen mask on before trying to help others! Mindfulness of body, mind and feelings are the ground from which a saner life can spring. But that doesn't mean our attention remains forever inward. Meditation is a practice – and we are practising for living our lives: doing our jobs, relating with family and friends, cultivating interests and, hopefully, developing our ability to live more happily and compassionately. By choosing to dedicate some time to formal meditation, we are creating suitable conditions in which to train our minds, so that we can be more present more often in our daily lives. It's like learning any other skill – you have to really work at it, in a training situation, before you can execute it with any kind of ease in less contained circumstances.

In the relatively structured environment of formal meditation, we learn to see our patterns of thinking and feeling, how we are impulsively driven to act those thoughts and feelings out, and we practise staying with our experience rather than being compelled by our need to 'do something'. Formal practice is just a step along the road to being able to execute the skill of mindfulness in the midst of our daily lives, with all their chaos, distractions and interruptions. When we begin to practise mindfulness in daily life, and not just in formal meditation, we are like a cyclist taking the stabilisers off her bike – having trained in maintaining our balance in supportive conditions, we are ready to try that same skill in circumstances that are more challenging. This is the essence of the fourth foundation of mindfulness: being mindful of all phenomena, which has sometimes been translated as 'mindfulness of life'. In this foundation we take the mindfulness we are developing and apply it to every aspect of our experience – not just our body, mind and feelings, but our close relationships, our work, our environment and our wider social interactions.

Mindfulness, then, is not about moving around slowly all the time, or passing our days in meditative absorption. In the long term it doesn't even necessarily mean 'doing less'; so long as we can continue to be mindful while we take action, we can go as fast as our mindfulness allows. It's possible, and sometimes desirable, to act quickly and decisively – and if we can be mindful at the same time, we may find ourselves actually performing at the height of our game, remaining in tune with our body and mind, and the world around us. As mindfulness trainer Michael Chaskalson points out, mindfulness is a quality exhibited by some of the greatest sports performers. 'Lewis Hamilton is mindful,' he says. 'Roger Federer is mindful.'

THE IMPACT OF ATTENTION

One particular quality of mindfulness is vital if we are to maintain it as we venture out into the world – attention. In Chapter 4, Kathy described telling her son that she was taking mindfulness classes to 'learn how to pay attention'. Similarly, Jon Kabat-Zinn, in his definition of mindfulness, refers to it as 'paying attention in a particular way'.[1] And Alan Wallace, author of *The Attention Revolution*, describes mindfulness as 'the quality of voluntarily sustaining one's attention on a chosen object'.[2]

In her book *Rapt: Attention and the Focused Life*, journalist Winifred Gallagher explores in great detail all the ways in which being able to choose what to pay attention to can have an impact on our lives. She describes how wellbeing comes not from being rich or famous, intelligent or good-looking, but mostly from being able to notice the things in life that we enjoy – when we lose that focus, we tend to revert to a default position of focusing on what is wrong rather than what is right.

It's a bit like the old story of the man who owns two dogs that are prone to get into fights with one another. Asked which dog usually wins the scrap, the man replies: 'The one I feed!' So it is with our attention – if we pay attention to the aspects of our lives that make us feel positive, we will become happier. If, on the other hand, we feed our negativity, we are more likely to lose heart.

The effect of focusing well can be significant – in a long-term study of nuns in the 20th century, it was found that, of the group of sisters who were most positive in their thinking styles, 90 per cent lived beyond the age of 58. Of another group who were the least cheerful, only 1 in 3 lived as long.[3] The promise of mindfulness is that, by repeatedly practising how to pay attention, we can get better at placing our minds on the things that are more likely to bring us happiness. This doesn't mean only ever thinking of positive things, or always trying to shut out or avoid unpleasant experiences. Actually, in some mindfulness practices we are encouraged to actively approach difficult thoughts, feelings and events, investigating with curiosity and courage how they are experienced in the body and mind. This then leads on to the 'C' in' Paramabandhu Groves' ABC model of mindfulness – having become aware of and learned to be with our internal experience, we can then make 'wise choices' about where and how to place our attention in the world at large. Alan Wallace sums up the importance of attention to living a good life: 'Whether it's playing football, working in an office, being a scientist, an artist, a professional chess player or a mother or father – if we engage in any meaningful activity at all without mindfulness, then we're incoherent and ineffective and our mind is dysfunctional.'

Researchers have carried out experiments to test whether meditation practices can indeed improve our attention skills – and it seems they can. At Penn University, Amishi Jha found that after a course of mindfulness-based stress reduction, people who had never meditated before showed a distinct improvement in their ability to focus.[4] Jha also discovered that experienced meditators who took part in a one-month retreat were more alert afterwards. Meanwhile,

Heleen Slagter has found that a three-month meditation training programme improves people's ability to detect visual cues that most of us wouldn't even notice – also suggesting that, after practising intensely, we are likely to perceive more of what is going on in the world around us.[5]

There's more – over at the University of Kentucky, Bruce O'Hara instructed a group of students to either meditate, sleep or watch television, before asking them to press a button when he flashed a light up on a screen – the students who had meditated reacted considerably faster, with those who had slept performing worst.[6] And at UCLA, Eileen Luders and her team found that the areas of the brain which are important for paying attention are larger in people who meditate compared to a set of control subjects with no meditation experience.[7] There seems little doubt that developing our mindfulness can improve our attention skills, and that improving our attention skills can enhance our experience of life.

TRY SOME AIMLESS WANDERING

One way to experience this simply and clearly is through the practice of 'aimless wandering'. A form of walking meditation, aimless wandering encourages us to let go of the 'get from A to B' goal-orientation that usually drives us when we are on the move, replacing it instead with a commitment simply to pay mindful attention to whatever is in our path. Just as when we pay attention to our thoughts, feelings and bodily sensations, we notice but don't judge them, so during aimless wandering we try simply to be curious about everything we encounter.

The instructions for aimless wandering are straightforward. Just stand up and start walking, slowly, in whatever direction the mood takes you (provided, of course, it's a safe place to go!). Notice any impulses to turn your wandering into a planned journey, any attempt to get somewhere, speed up or fulfil a particular task – beyond simply experiencing your aimless wander in a mindful way. Each time you feel any such impulses, bring your mind back to your experience – not just your bodily sensations, thoughts and feelings, but also the environment around you.

When you remove the 'doing' aspect of your relationship with the world, how does this change your experience of it? By placing your attention fully on a parked car, rather than rushing past it, do you notice aspects of it that would otherwise have gone unseen? Scratches on its bodywork, reflections in its windows, a broken windscreen wiper, a personalised number plate, a parking ticket? Is it possible to find each of these elements interesting and curious, even though they might otherwise have seemed mundane, or have gone unnoticed? By coming into a 'being' mode of operation, are we not more able to take satisfaction in, and even be fascinated by, the apparently humdrum? Do we really need so much of the stimulation we usually seek to keep us occupied?

You can practise aimless wandering in the city, in the park, in remote rural areas, or at the beach – anywhere you have the freedom to take a directionless walk. You can practise for 10 minutes, half an hour or longer – as long as you can sustain attention on the world around you in a way that takes in your environment mindfully rather than ignoring it in favour of 'getting somewhere'.

Aimless wandering is, of course, another formal meditation practice. But once we have a flavour of a mindful mode of relating to the world outside, we can go much further. We can start to move towards integrating our developing mindfulness – our ability to let go, allow, accept and be – with the activities that are inevitably required for us to function in the world. Far from being an escape, mindfulness meditation is actually a gateway to being able to work more skilfully with any situations that we encounter.

ACT

The mindful attitude to working with everyday life is neatly encapsulated in the name given to another new form of psychological treatment – Acceptance and Commitment Therapy (known as ACT for short).

The *acceptance* part of ACT reflects the importance of the first three foundations of mindfulness. If we are to make skilful responses in our lives rather than simply following skewed perceptions and unenlightened impulses, we need to be able to check in with our bodies, minds and feelings, using mindfulness to understand how they influence our experience. We can then practise accepting that experience when it is unpleasant or difficult, and minimise the amount of extra suffering we create in reaction to it. If all we do is accept our experience, however, then nothing much changes. The second part of ACT is *commitment* – the willingness to engage in behaviour that may improve our situation. Having increased our awareness and practised accepting whatever we encounter, the action we take

can be guided by our own basic intelligence, based on
the information we receive from our bodies, minds and
emotions. There is no set formula for what this action
will be – each situation is different – but it's always based
on touching in with our inherent wisdom, and allowing
ourselves to trust that, when we are able mindfully to make
a connection with ourselves and the circumstances we are
facing, we can act wisely.

Imagine that you are faced with a difficult colleague at
work. You feel that he is constantly criticising you unfairly,
putting down your abilities, minimising your achievements
and denting your confidence. How might such a situation
affect you? Touch in with mindfulness of body, mind and
feelings to get a sense of how you feel when you visualise
this scenario. Do you feel a knot in your stomach, a boiling
of the blood? What are your thoughts – do you find yourself
believing the criticisms, or mentally attacking the colleague
with put-downs of your own? Do you feel angry, frightened
or helpless?

Now, having taken your internal temperature in this way,
ask yourself: 'What should I do in this situation? What
is the best way for me to respond?' There is no one right
answer – it will inevitably depend on your own personality,
that of the critical colleague, your work situation, the
attitude of your boss and many other variables. But, by
approaching the situation in a mindful way rather than
instinctively reacting without contemplation, you stand
a greater chance of making a good decision. We are
being mindful of life, rather than living on automatic
pilot. Training in connecting with our internal wellbeing

increases our ability to respond skilfully to the conflicts, demands and pressures that inevitably come our way.

Mindfulness means acceptance *and* commitment, letting go *and* taking action. These are not the contradictory strategies they might sound, but instead reflect a potentially harmonious integration of the 'being' and 'doing' modes of living. Learning how to *be* actually makes what we *do* more effective and fulfilling.

MINDFULNESS FOR LIFE

Mindfulness, then, is meant to be applied to life itself – to our work, to our relationships, to how we bring up our children. If we restrict it to a daily practice session, then we are more than slightly missing the point. The most profound reason for cultivating mindfulness is so that we can apply it to every situation we face, potentially transforming and enriching our experience in the process. How would it be if we were able to be mindful when we were stuck on a train, having an argument, enjoying a beautiful sunset, playing Scrabble, doing the washing up, going for a run, attending a funeral, at the dentist's or in a boring six-hour meeting? Could it actually enhance our experience of these situations, and enable us to meet them more wisely? Could it allow us to deepen every experience rather than splashing around on the surface?

Far from being about passively avoiding the world, meditation offers a foundation for going forward to meet the challenges of living with greater awareness and greater confidence that we have the skills to cope with those challenges. It trains us in a different way of relating to our internal and external experiences as they appear to us in the present moment – a way that actually amounts to facing them head on, right now. We can both accept reality, and act in flow with it.

This is where the potential for mindfulness to have an impact on our world goes way beyond the confines of 'self-help'. Instead, mindfulness is a tool that takes us out of the limitations of self – by connecting us to a wider view, showing us how our experience interrelates with that of others, and with our environment, it can help us start to build a more harmonious world. This is true if we are the only person in our community practising mindfulness – in which case we are more able to see our own habitual patterns, and less likely to react unskilfully and impulsively when others press our buttons – but it could be especially true if groups of people commit to practising. When more than one person becomes able to respond with awareness, it can make a big difference to the whole energy of that environment – instead of everyone contributing their habitual patterns to a set of predictable chain reactions, there is the potential for transformation, a conscious change in the status quo based on mindful awareness and considered decision-making.

Let's take the world of work as an example. According to the UK Health and Safety Executive, one in five employees reports feeling 'very' or 'extremely' stressed in his job, while depression and anxiety are the cause of 13 million lost working days every year.[8] Since the mid-1990s, the number of people who say their stress was either caused by or made worse by their jobs has doubled, and the cost of work-related stress to the UK has been estimated at £3.7 billion a year. Demanding bosses, difficult projects, pressure to succeed, interpersonal problems with co-workers – the potential for stress at work is enormous, and affects most of us at some time or another.

TACKLING STRESS AT WORK

We've already seen how mindfulness is an effective treatment for stress in healthcare settings. And there is now some suggestion that teaching people how to be mindful can help them cope better at work. Take Transport for London, a company which employs over 20,000 people who work on the English capital's tube and bus network.[9] As any of us who travel in big cities at rush hour know, commuting environments can be stressful places – and this is especially true for those who work all day in them. So it is perhaps not surprising that an internal review by Transport for London in 2003 found that mental health problems were one of the top two health issues resulting in employees being off sick.

To tackle the problem, TfL developed a strategy to help staff deal more effectively with stress – as part of it, they started offering a six-week workshop to help employees who were struggling. The course combines the teaching of mindfulness techniques with cognitive behavioural therapy, and it seems to have been a great success. Among those employees who took the course, days off sick due to stress, depression and anxiety fell by over 70 per cent in the following three years (absences for all health conditions were halved). Interestingly, participants on the course reported improvements not just in their stress levels, but also in their quality of life – 80 per cent said their relationships had got better, 79 per cent said they were more able to relax, and 53 per cent said they were happier in their jobs. Emerald-Jane Turner, who developed the course, says that participants often report using the techniques in their personal as well as their work lives. 'Participants learn that they have some control over their responses, even if they can't control the events themselves – what a customer says to them, for example. And people take it home with them – they'll say things like: "When I'm on the phone with my ex-wife, I can step back instead of having a go at her." The breakthroughs that people have are sometimes quite extraordinary.'

In another small study done in Sweden, where 14 per cent of the population who are of working age are unable to work due to sickness or disability, Joanne Dahl and her colleagues looked at using Acceptance and Commitment Therapy with a group of public health sector workers who showed chronic stress or pain and were, therefore, at high risk of taking time off sick.[10] Participants were divided into two groups and either offered ACT or their usual medical treatment. While the results did not show significant differences between the groups in their levels of pain or stress, the group who received ACT had fewer sick days and used fewer medical resources in the six months following their treatment.

Mindfulness may be especially useful for business leaders, not just for stress management (three-quarters of executives say that stress affects their health, happiness and home life, as well as their work performance[11]) but also for promoting the kind of 'mindful leadership' that might permeate through an entire organisation, positively affecting the way a company operates. According to the business school INSEAD, access to meditation-based executive coaching programmes makes it more likely that managers will act in a socially responsible way.[12]

Michael Chaskalson, who has run 'mindful leadership' training in the UK Government Cabinet and Home Offices, as well as for companies such as KPMG, PricewaterhouseCoopers and the Prudential, agrees: 'By developing greater awareness, you can enjoy better relationships with your colleagues, be more able to renew yourself from stress, and develop your attention. You can't have too much mindfulness – whatever the problem is, if you're better able to work with the content of your mind, things will go better for you.'

This seems to be borne out by research – in a UK trial of Acceptance and Commitment Therapy delivered in a company setting, participants not only enjoyed better mental health, but their ability to be creative also improved – perhaps a result of being able to stand back from problems and view them from the 'bigger picture' perspective that mindfulness can offer.[13]

Those whose jobs involve caring for others could particularly benefit from mindfulness. By fostering an attentive, non-judgemental attitude, mindfulness can bring out a person's ability to be compassionate, to listen and to respond skilfully to people in distress, without becoming

so caught up in others' difficulties that they burn out
emotionally themselves. Those in the helping professions
are often acutely aware of their need for tools which can
help them deal more skilfully with the situations that
come up in their work. In a US study, a year-long course
for doctors which incorporated mindfulness training was
offered to 70 GPs, and the results were studied by Michael
Krasner at the University of Rochester.[14] Krasner found that
the course not only reduced burnout and exhaustion, but
also increased the physicians' ability to be empathetic with
their patients. And an earlier study by Dr Shauna Shapiro
and her colleagues at the University of Arizona looked at
the effects of putting medical students through an eight-
week meditation course.[15] They too found that this not only
reduced the stress and anxiety felt by the students, but also
increased their ability to empathise with patients. This is
important – empathy is a key part of a doctor's 'bedside
manner', and not only does it make a big difference to
patients' experience, but it may even affect their recovery
prospects.

Actually, it's hard to think of any job that could not be done
better if we applied ourselves to it with mindfulness. Police
officers might notice details of a case that would otherwise
be missed, journalists might be more able to listen to
their interviewees, understand their own motivation and
biases, and create a more balanced and accurate account
of a story, teachers might better be able to let go of their
own emotional reactions to a difficult class and continue to
respond attentively to the students in their care, and lorry
drivers could drive more safely as they pay greater attention
to their vehicle, their cargo and fellow road users.

Can you see how practising all the foundations of
mindfulness – body, mind, feelings and life – could change
the way you do your own job, whatever it might be? If you
work with others, how might promoting mindfulness in
your organisation improve creativity, productivity and
camaraderie? Just as importantly, how could it enable you
to manage your own stress better? In a distracted world
where we are all having to cope with rapidly changing
technology and 24-hour communication via email and
mobile phones, we have to find a way to take care of
ourselves, and maintain a sense of balance and equilibrium
in our lives. Mindfulness can help us see situations as they
are, manage our uncertainty, deal with disappointment and
free us up to make imaginative, intelligent decisions – all
qualities that will allow us not only to perform well at work,
but also to flourish in every aspect of our lives.

GOOGLING MEDITATION

**Search engine giants Google are just one of the
increasing number of organisations that are
offering meditation training to employees.**

Over the last few years, Google has developed
a mindfulness-based emotional intelligence
training programme open to staff at its California
headquarters. The programme was inspired by
Chade-Meng Tan, a Google executive who believes
that more widespread practice of meditation is key
to creating a better world. Google already operates

what might be considered a mindful approach to office life – as well as working in a spacious, relaxed environment, Google staff are encouraged to spend one day a week working on a self-generated project that interests them, in the expectation that allowing such free-flowing creativity is most likely to lead to the innovation for which the company is renowned.

However, this attitude has been taken one step further by the creation of the company's Search Inside Yourself programme, which aims to help staff create and enjoy an even more mindful ambience. The course presents meditation as a mental technology based on scientific principles and as a way to exercise the mind, just as physical exercise offers a workout for the body. As well as lectures from eminent speakers in the meditation field, there is practical training – six weekly two-hour meditation sessions, plus a one-day retreat. Participants are also offered tips on how to adopt a more contemplative approach to their jobs – how to listen mindfully to colleagues for example, or send mindful emails.

THE MINDFUL CHILD

But why should we wait until adulthood to teach people mindfulness skills? If we really want to embed the benefits that meditative disciplines can bring to individuals and to society, shouldn't we prioritise the teaching of basic mindfulness practices in early life? Several initiatives have already been developed to enable children to experience the fruits of mindfulness practice. In the UK, the Oxford Mindfulness Centre has pioneered a schools programme to be delivered by local teachers as part of the SEAL (Social and Emotional Aspects of Learning) curriculum. Mark Williams, the director of the Centre, says that young people are often open to being taught mindfulness skills – 'as soon as they try to meditate, they realise it's hard, so it's a challenge. They can become quite curious as to why it's so difficult to keep your mind focused.' And in the US, mindfulness practices are taught to students through initiatives such as the Los Angeles-based InnerKids foundation, with research showing that even very young children with attention problems are more able to focus once they have been taught the techniques. There is also an adaptation of the eight-week mindfulness course – mindfulness-based cognitive therapy for children (MBCT-C) that is specially designed to present mindfulness skills in ways and doses that are age-appropriate – as with its adult counterparts, early research suggests it may significantly reduce problems such as anxiety and depression, as well as attention span difficulties.[16]

At a time when it's estimated that up to 5 per cent of school-age children in England and Wales qualify for a diagnosis of Attention Deficit Hyperactivity Disorder (ADHD) (420,000 prescriptions for drugs to treat ADHD were issued to under-16s in 2007)[17] wouldn't an approach to wellbeing that explicitly fosters the ability to pay attention more effectively be of some use, not just to these children but to *all* students, whose ability to learn is intimately related to their capacity for paying attention?

If teaching mindfulness can make such significant differences to people when they are adults, wouldn't the impact be much greater if the training were offered earlier in life, before our habitual patterns of reacting impulsively to our thoughts and feelings become so ingrained? A review of mindfulness-based interventions for children and adolescents seems to suggest that this might be the case – a 2009 paper by Christine Burke, published in the *Journal of Child and Family Studies*, lists positive results from studies with children from pre-school-age upwards.[18]

Some researchers are attempting to intervene even earlier. Mark Williams enthuses about the potential for mindfulness-based childbirth and parenting programmes, and the Oxford Mindfulness Centre, together with US nurse and midwife Nancy Bardake, are exploring the potential for mindfulness to help pregnant women and their partners cope with the stresses of having children. Williams suggests that pregnancy classes offer a great opportunity for mindfulness training because 'when you're about to have a baby is the one time you'll accept class-based training without feeling pathologised – you turn up because you're scared. You want to get information and do the best by your child.' Based on the existing evidence for mindfulness interventions, Williams and his colleagues hope that teaching parents-to-be mindfulness skills will help them deal with the fear and pain associated with childbirth, reduce the likelihood of postnatal depression, and enable both parents to form good bonds with their children. A pilot study of a mindfulness programme for pregnant women has already shown promise – reducing anxiety and depression compared to mothers-to-be in control groups who did not receive the treatment.[19]

MINDFUL RELATIONSHIPS

Work, schooling, parenting – each is an aspect of life that usually requires some skill in relationships, and which appears to be enhanced by a mindful approach. But what about relationships themselves? Can being mindful make a direct difference to our interpersonal connections? From studies that rate people's mindfulness using questionnaires, and then ask them about their lives, we know that more mindful people enjoy more satisfying relationships, are better at communicating and are less troubled by conflict in their relationships, as well as being less likely to think negatively of their partners as a result of conflict.[20] They also express themselves better in social situations, are more empathic and can identify and describe their feelings more accurately. And they are less likely to experience social anxiety, or to be affected when people around them are distressed. There are correlations between mindfulness and 'emotional intelligence', the possession of which is linked to strong social skills, the ability to co-operate and to see things from another person's perspective. People who are more mindful are also less likely to react defensively when threatened.

Daniel Siegel, author of *The Mindful Brain*, describes mindfulness as 'a form of intrapersonal attunement' – learning how to be mindful gives us the ability to see our own mind.[21] Because we can see our own mind, he suggests, we also become more adept at seeing and understanding other people's minds. And when we can understand others, we are more likely to be able to relate to them with compassion and empathy – we feel we know, at least to some extent, what they are going through because we also experience difficulties with our own minds. Not only that, but because mindfulness means not judging ourselves, we learn to refrain from seeing the people around us in terms of 'good' and 'bad' – we simply see them, without giving in to our tendency to think we are always right and they are always wrong. Rather than setting ourselves up to attack others, or defend ourselves from them when we are attacked, we create the potential for a more open form of interpersonal communication – one based more on dialogue and a meeting of minds rather than a fight.

Mindfulness seems to enhance relationships in several other ways, too. It helps us pay attention to another person – a vital ingredient to any effective relationship. Because we each of us see the world in a unique way, to develop good relationships we have to be willing to pay attention to how others perceive things differently. As if our own distorted view of reality is not complicated enough, when we then add someone else's perception, which may be just as skewed as our own, the potential for confusion doubles. By being mindful of these differences when we relate with others, we increase the likelihood of noticing when it is *our* perceptions that are leading to conflict, and of being able to stay with our own discomfort rather than blaming somebody else for it.

So, perhaps, rather than getting angry with our partner for withdrawing from us, we might remember that this is just her habitual response when she feels hurt or something is worrying her, and we can make a mindful decision to approach her with extra love and care rather than pressure and frustration. Meanwhile, she may know that when we feel anxious we get irritable, and can make the extra effort to come towards us, even when she feels like withdrawing.

Mindful of our patterns, we can cut through interactions that might have become furious arguments, and turn them instead into conversations that bring us closer to our loved one. We can move towards our partner, demonstrating that we have heard and understood his perspective, and then work together to find a way forward which, as far as possible, meets both of our needs.

This kind of accepting, compassionate, inquisitive communication is at the heart of mindfulness-based relationship enhancement (MBRE), another adaptation of MBSR that aims to help couples improve their interaction with each other and deal more effectively with relationship stress. As well as the kinds of meditation exercises that form the core of all mindfulness-based interventions, MBRE places particular emphasis on mindful communication to develop empathy, trust and intimacy between participants, who attend as couples. According to research into the programme carried out by James Carson at the University of North Carolina, MBRE improves couples' relationship satisfaction, their levels of closeness and their acceptance of each other, and decreases their levels of relationship distress.[22] The ability to let go and be present which mindfulness cultivates is even being used to enhance people's sex lives – one study has found that women who practise mindfulness report greater arousal and better orgasms, and the approach is recommended by staff at the sexual dysfunction unit in St Mary's Hospital in London. Perhaps unsurprisingly, you can now buy a book on the subject, called *The Joy of Mindful Sex*![23]

JANE'S EXPERIENCE

Jane, 52, is a company chief executive in London. She heard about mindfulness from a coach she was seeing at work – she had just taken on her first job as a CEO and she was finding it tough. 'I'd never run a business before so it was a steep learning curve,' she explains, 'When I took the job, the company was going bust. I hadn't realised what I had taken on and I was stressed out of my skull – I'm also a single parent – and I needed some support and a way to relax.'

As part of her company package, Jane had a small training budget that she was allowed to spend on anything she wanted. She decided to sign up for a course of mindfulness-based cognitive therapy. 'The course was fantastic, I loved it. I can take the messages, like "thoughts are not facts," and reinforce them in myself. I get really strongly that you don't have to go where your mind takes you.

Instead of that whole conveyor belt of resentment and anger which I could get caught up in forever when I was younger, I can recognise it and listen to it but not go down that road.' She says that with mindfulness, she is now more able to manage the pressures of work. 'I am much calmer in the office, much more positive – even though my job can still be very stressful.'

Jane has also found mindfulness to be a powerful aid in her personal life. 'At first I thought that meditation might just calm me down. But then I started reading about mindfulness for depression and it became much bigger, much more useful. I was really depressed for five years after my partner left me with a young child. I went into therapy, and it feels like mindfulness has added to all that work. Since the course, my ex and I have become much better friends and been nicer to each other, so I think it helped in the very difficult healing of that relationship. And because I feel much better and can take care of myself, I can also help people around me.'

As someone whose parents died when she was young, the idea that mindfulness might be a way of self-parenting is something that strikes a chord for Jane. 'One of my big patterns is feeling abandoned – especially if I haven't got someone to see or something to do. But I can go upstairs to meditate and that feeling of abandonment just disappears. It definitely feels like a way of parenting yourself, rather than getting someone else to do it for you. After the course I can say that I don't feel abandoned, I don't feel depressed and I'm managing things better. I feel like I can take care of myself, whereas before I often didn't want to.'

Although she herself puts a lot of effort into taking care of her mental health, Jane doesn't think most people are aware of the importance of managing their minds, especially in the often frenetic environment of big cities. 'People go to the gym, and they think about what they eat, but they don't often think: "I need to take care of my emotional health." Speaking as a Londoner, I think we live in quite a hostile world – but mindfulness shows us how to take note of the positive – like when there's a pleasant exchange in a shop or in the street. There was an exercise on the course where you practise taking note of pleasant experiences – I like that, deciding to notice the nice things in life.'

Mindfulness is a skill that can be of benefit in any life situation, because rather than trying to change the circumstances themselves, primarily it means changing the way we relate to those circumstances. Of course, it may be that the situation will change as a result of our approaching it in a different way, but even if our situation remains difficult, the very fact of our relating to it mindfully can make a difference. As Mark Williams puts it: 'It doesn't mean you won't lose your glasses, and it doesn't mean you won't ever lose your temper with children, partners or parents – but there is just a chance that the aftermath will be more skilfully handled.'

A MINDFUL WORLD

In this book we have gradually expanded the domain of our mindfulness outwards. We started by paying attention to our breathing, and then increased our awareness to take into account our bodies, our thoughts, our feelings, and then finally every aspect of our experience – such as our relationships with the people around us, at work, at school or at home. But this expansion can be taken even further – the potential for mindfulness to have an impact on our world is limited only by the capacity of people to try it, embrace it and keep developing it as a skill. As we described in Chapter 1, if enough people take up mindfulness meditation, it has the potential to change the world. This won't happen overnight – our habitual patterns are too ingrained for that – but gradually, over time, we could start to enjoy living in a society that embodies mindful principles. Such a society might be more compassionate, more insightful, less speedy and less reactive, with each practitioner's ever-developing mindfulness contributing to the whole. Rather than being dominated by unreflective 'doing', this society would start also to manifest 'being' – a mode of mind in which we are more able to slow down, notice what is going on and respond in a way that promotes harmony rather than conflict.

The possibilities are limited only by our imaginations. We have already seen how mindfulness can be used to help us

cope with so many of the seemingly intractable problems
that afflict our world – from chronic physical illness to
depression, addiction and all kinds of life stress. Why not
then enlarge the domain of mindful attention to the very
widest level: to the problems which afflict us not just at an
individual or local level, but nationally and internationally?
As Mark Williams says, 'Lack of mindfulness is involved
in all the major issues that we deal with – everything from
crime to international relations.'

Just as slowing down and noticing more can help us
negotiate our physical and mental health, our emotions
and our daily lives with greater awareness and skill, taking
a meditative approach to the problems that afflict us
collectively could reap the same benefits. These global issues
– poverty, environmental abuse, or war – may seem like
insoluble problems because of their magnitude, but they are
at their root created and sustained by the same automatic,
mindless patterns of thinking, feeling and behaving that
motivate us as individuals and which, as we have seen,
can start to be understood, withstood and countered
with mindfulness. It will not be a miracle cure for all our
problems – believing that would be to fall into the same
speedy, quick-fix-desiring trap that we are already in – but
it would be a healthy beginning with which we could start
to acknowledge, accept and, gradually, reverse the trends
that have led us into so much trouble.

Can you imagine then, a mindful media, where newspapers,
magazines and TV choose which stories to cover based not
on their capacity for appealing to our impulses of greed,
fear or anger, but because they will truly inform us about

the state of our world, and help awaken our awareness and compassion? Or a mindful approach to climate change, where governments were really prepared to be aware of, stay with and choose to forgo short-term self-interest in order to form an approach to the planetary crisis that will benefit everyone in the longer term? Or a mindful parliamentary system where, instead of shouting at each other over the dispatch box, politicians worked together to find the most workable approaches to government? The mindful model of society is one of collaboration rather than competition – rather than fighting with one another to be better, faster, richer or more admired, we can take note of how our tendency to compete does not lead to greater happiness, for ourselves or anyone else, and then commit to behaving differently.

Putting this model into effect may seem a long way off, and perhaps it is – but there could surely be no harm in calling on those in positions of influence to explore the practice of mindfulness meditation for themselves, and to encourage its collective practice wherever possible – a short period of meditation could precede business meetings, or the days' proceedings at political conferences, for instance. In a world overrun by activity, such small gestures towards 'being' could well prove to be more helpful than yet another plan or pledge that focuses on telling us what we want to hear rather than how things actually are.

Wherever there is more mindfulness, there is greater possibility for awareness, patience, kindness, wisdom and courage to flourish. And wherever those qualities are manifested, skilful action is more likely to emerge.

MAINSTREAM MINDFULNESS

What, then, can we all do to help this process along? Throughout this book we have offered suggestions, explanations, practices, and tips designed to help you begin your own mindfulness practice. We hope these have helped get you started, but while books are helpful, if you want to develop your practice further, it is highly recommended that you seek out a qualified instructor and a supportive community of practitioners – mindfulness is a direct experience rather than a concept, so there is a limit to what you can learn by reading books alone.

As mindfulness meditation becomes more mainstream, there are an increasing number of courses being offered across the country by teachers trained in mindfulness-based approaches. The Mental Health Foundation has a dedicated mindfulness website (bemindful.co.uk) which lists many of these courses, and you can also try an internet search for mindfulness + your local area, to see what is available near you.

As mindfulness starts to become more accepted as a valuable healthcare intervention, an increasing number of GPs are able to refer patients (especially those with recurrent depression) to MBCT courses. If you think you might qualify, ask your GP what is available – if there is nothing nearby, contact your local Primary Care Trust and lobby them to provide MBCT courses, which, you might want to point out, are a recommended NHS treatment for people with repeated episodes of depression.

If you are attracted to the Buddhist tradition, there are Buddhist meditation groups in most towns and cities, often offering free or inexpensive evening or weekend sessions. There are also retreat centres (such as Gaia House in Devon, http://www.gaiahouse.co.uk/) which offer an extensive residential programme of meditation for those who feel inclined to deepen their practice further. Alternatively, you could start a mindfulness group yourself – if there is no one available with teaching experience, there are a range of excellent CDs and podcasts available which offer guided instruction from mindfulness experts, including the developers of mindfulness-based stress reduction (Jon Kabat-Zinn, http://www.mindfulnesstapes.com/) and mindfulness-based cognitive therapy (Mark Williams, http://mbct.co.uk/cd-set/). We are also producing a range of audio materials to guide you through the practices described in this book – to find out more, please visit our website at www.themindfulmanifesto.com.

The essence of mindfulness of life is a natural expansion from its beginnings in practices centred on the body and mind of the individual, to a wider view based on understanding the interdependence and connection that exists between all of us. Far from being selfish, mindfulness practice is one of the most compassionate, community-centred things we can do.

PRACTICE: Mini-meditation for Daily Life

As our practice develops, we can start to road-test it, approaching more and more life situations in a mindful way. As John Teasdale has said, mindfulness isn't hard – it's *remembering* to be mindful that's difficult. Just as in our formal practice the mind can sometimes drift away from the object of our meditation again and again, so we are prone to forget to keep paying mindful attention when we get into the swing of our lives. However, just as we bring our attention back to the breath or the body when this happens in practice, in mindfulness of life we simply note what has happened, come back to the situation we are facing, and gently bring mindfulness to it once more.

One way to develop this is to practise the following mini-meditation that covers each of the four foundations of mindfulness in turn – body, mind, feelings, and then environment – spending a few moments on each step (the whole thing could take anything from 30 seconds to five minutes or longer). It can be practised wherever you are – at your desk, on a train or bus, or in a supermarket queue.

At first it may be good to practise this at set times, perhaps several times a day, so you can get used to bringing yourself into awareness while in the middle of activities (you could set the alarm on your phone to remind you). You can also use it when you are faced with a particularly challenging situation, those times when we are more likely to fall back into being on automatic pilot, and into habitual patterns of thinking or behaving that don't serve us well. It helps us instantly ground ourselves with awareness, creating space from which we can choose to respond more skilfully.

STEP ONE
Take a relaxed, upright, dignified posture. Whether standing or sitting, manifest with your body a sense of

being confident, present and awake. If you want, close your eyes. Now, place your attention on your breathing. Notice the rising and falling of your chest and abdomen as you inhale and exhale. Feel your awareness connect with the breath as it moves in and out, again and again. Allow your mind to ride the breath, feeling its power as it takes you along, gently aligning yourself with its movement and energy.

STEP TWO
Next, allow yourself to connect with what is happening in your body. Become aware of your whole body – and any sensations you may be experiencing in it right now. If the sensations are unpleasant, see if you can approach them kindly, inviting them in and greeting them with friendliness, even when the instinct is to push them away.

STEP THREE
Now, move your attention to your thoughts. Notice what is going through your mind – watch your thoughts as they come into your awareness, pass through and fall away. Again, rather than attaching to or judging the thoughts, just accept them as they are. Be curious about your experience and kind to yourself as you are observing it. 'Aha, this is what my mind is doing right now – I see.' Perhaps even chuckle to yourself as you recognise familiar patterns.

STEP FOUR
Next, turn your attention to your emotions. Are you feeling joy, sadness, anger, fear – or some combination of these? How are these feelings expressing themselves in your body at the moment? Where do you feel them?

STEP FIVE

Finally, expand your awareness to take in the whole of your experience, including your immediate environment. What can you see, hear, smell? How are your body, mind and feelings interacting with your present moment life situation – the physical space around you, the people nearby, the activities you are undertaking today. Feel your breath, your body, your mind, your feelings and your environment, all in awareness together.

STEP SIX

As you come out of the mini-meditation, now ask yourself, 'What is the most skilful thing for me to do right now?' Try to be genuine and listen to the response that comes from your heart before carrying on with your day. In this way tap into your experience, notice what is happening in a non-critical way and allow your inherent wisdom to guide you in any difficult situation you face.

MINDFULNESS OF LIFE: SUGGESTIONS FOR PRACTICE

Here are a few more suggestions for making your experience of everyday life more mindful …

KEEP COMING BACK TO FORMAL PRACTICE

No matter how skilful we become at being mindful in daily life, it is important to keep coming back to the more structured meditation practices, reserving a small portion of each day for practice, if we can. Just as we need to keep exercising if we want to remain fit, so maintaining a regular formal mindfulness practice helps us maintain our ability to be mindful the rest of the time. But don't beat yourself up if you fall out of practice for a while – just notice it, and see if you can make a fresh start, without judging yourself.

TRAIN WITH EVERYDAY ACTIVITIES

A good way of developing mindfulness of life skills is to practise being mindful while engaging in activities you usually do on automatic pilot. Make a conscious attempt to stay mindful while washing the dishes, going for a run, driving in traffic, having a bath, getting dressed or doing the vacuuming. You might find that paying attention to these everyday activities can radically change the way you experience them. Mindfully washing the dishes, for example, can turn a humdrum task into a vivid sensory experience (noticing the softness of the soap suds on your hands, appreciating the change from dirty to clean plates, experiencing the feeling of a job done well).

USE DIFFICULT SITUATIONS AS A MINDFUL CHALLENGE

It can be tempting to think that some situations are just too tough for us to practise mindfulness in – our circumstances are too noisy, too chaotic, too overwhelming, too painful. But no matter how hard the situation, is it likely to be more or less difficult for us if we are mindful or mindless? The important thing is to stay with the practice, and not judge ourselves for 'failing' – indeed, our practice is a success simply by virtue of the fact that we have remembered to engage in it. We do the best we can, and then congratulate ourselves for that.

DEVELOP MINDFULNESS CUES

Traditionally, gongs and bells signal the start of a meditation session – can you turn the sounds of modern life into your reminders to be mindful? Get into the habit of coming back to mindfulness every time your phone rings, or you hear the sound of a car, or you switch your computer on, or your alarm goes off in the morning.

GO AT THE SPEED AT WHICH YOU CAN STAY MINDFUL

The Mindful Manifesto is about doing less and noticing more. But it is not about 'going slow' – if, like great sportspeople, you can be mindful at speed, then by all means go at that pace. Notice what speed of life you can handle mindfully, and see if you can cultivate a life that can support you living at that pace.

Jonty's Experience

GPs are very lucky, and don't let anyone tell you otherwise! We have one of the most fulfilling jobs it is possible to have, and yet a quarter of GPs plan to retire early – and, of these, a third cite stress as the reason. I have only been in general practice for just over 10 years and I love it, but I have no doubt that the pressures it places me under are significant. Attending to people is hard work. Sometimes we don't appreciate just how generous our friends and family are being when they simply listen to us. Truly placing our attention onto someone else for a time is demanding – staying with them, listening not just to what they are saying but also to what they are not saying, and then trying to help them with whatever difficulty they are dealing with is a pretty big ask – particularly if you are doing that for 30–40 people a day. If you then add to that the usual demands of running a business, looking after staff, maintaining the premises and all this while constant change is imposed on you from above, you can see that the pressures are high – particularly if, like me, you don't deal well with uncertainty!

I have no doubt that my need for perfection and my relative rigidity make coping with these demands more difficult. Like many doctors, I like to solve problems – whether they are my patients' or my own. Like a dog with a bone I find it very difficult to let go of whatever is bothering me. My shower in the morning is usually spent ruminating over issues at work, and I am renowned for staying late at the practice, trying to make sure that I have finished all my tasks for the day. While this does not sound like much fun, in and of itself it may not be a huge problem – apart from missing out on the joy of a hot shower or the chance to watch *Eastenders* in the evening! But, of course, it doesn't stop there. My drive for perfection extends to my expectations of others, it leads to frustration and criticism, and this potentially damages my relationships with friends, family, work colleagues and even patients.

At work, mindfulness helps me not only to attend to my patients in a more genuine way but also to notice how my coping mechanisms contribute to my own stress and that of the people around me. Gradually I have become more aware of the ripples I create in my life, both internal and external, and while change is, as has already been said, not easy, at least by becoming (in a non-critical way) more aware of how I contribute to this stress, I give myself the chance to do things differently.

Ed's Experience

In Buddhism there's a long tradition of hermit practitioners – people who go off and spend their lives meditating on their own. It's considered a noble thing to do – you are working on your mind so you can develop greater compassion. However, it's also believed by many that you aren't enlightened until you've learned how to use your practice to help others. I can also sometimes use meditation as a bit of an escape from life – how luxurious to spend time on my own, in the quiet, paying attention to my breath, rather than be out dealing with the chaos of the modern world. But I also know that much of the joy of life comes from relating with others – my extrovert side loves to be around people. Sometimes that means being willing to approach rather than hide from difficult situations and tolerate – even welcome – the unpleasant experiences that can arise.

Being mindful in relationships feels like a real challenge, but a worthwhile one. It doesn't, as I used to imagine, mean talking more slowly, or trying to dull my sometimes sharp sense of humour. It does mean doing my best to recognise that I am not always right, and that my relationships work better when I am willing to listen to the other person's point of view, and not treat it as a threat. Mindfulness in relationships for me means lightening up, loosening up and laughing at myself a bit more often.

It's important for me to remember the commitment aspect to mindfulness. Just because I have learned to meditate doesn't change the fact that I have to motivate myself to act – but my hope is that more often I'm able to check in with myself and choose to behave in ways that are less damaging, and more helpful to myself and everyone else I come across. It's a constant work in progress ...

CONCLUSION

Mindfulness is not a cure for our pain, but it allows us to wake up from the anaesthetic of activity we have created and really experience our lives – every time we forget this, our breath is there to remind us that we are alive.

How does it feel to 'be' now, compared to when we asked you to experiment with it back in Chapter 1? Try the practice again – put down this book for two minutes and, wherever you are, just be there, without following any particular meditation technique.

What was your experience this time? Able to manage it without any difficulty now? (Based on our experience, this seems unlikely!) Or was it exactly the same as when you tried it the first time (equally unlikely)? The chances are that while you may well experience many similar states of mind, body, feelings and life as before, perhaps you are able to relate to them slightly differently?

If you have now practised mindfulness meditation for a while, there's a possibility that you won't be so heavily *identified* with your pain, your thoughts, your emotions or your environment. Perhaps you might be a little more aware of how they come up in your experience, and how you can relate to them in a way that creates a little less suffering for yourself and for others? Perhaps you might be a touch more gentle, a touch more compassionate, a touch less self-critical? Perhaps you might be able to stay with your experience a little longer, without reacting so impulsively? Perhaps you might see a way forward in your life that's based on holding your experience in mindful awareness and making wise decisions from that position of greater clarity and strength?

The practice of 'just being' can follow on naturally from each of the practices we have explored in this book. Sometimes we might start with a period of being mindful of our breath, body, mind, feelings or life, and then, once settled, we can move into a more formless practice, letting go of any object of attention and simply allowing ourselves to be open to and engaged with all of our direct experiences – we simply 'are', in the present moment, experiencing the world as it is.

This does not mean that our experience is necessarily blissful, or even pleasant, or that the usual whirr of sensations, thoughts, feelings and incidents does not occur – this is just another practice, after all – but by dropping any specific meditation technique, we are connecting to a more expansive mode of experience – one that doesn't replace doing, but which can balance it, enabling our lives to be gradually less stretched, less distracted and more whole. With that can come a feeling of greater peace, warmth, love, equanimity and joy.

A WAY OF BEING

Mindfulness doesn't solve all our problems – but it does offer us a way of being with them. This way of being is based on self-care rather than self-improvement, compassion rather than judgement. As we start paying more attention to what we are thinking, saying and doing, as we start to notice how we are feeling in a non-judgemental way, we can start to soften towards ourselves and others. Our self-commentary can become less harsh and less critical, and we can start to take a more kindly interest in ourselves and the world around us.

Some interesting recent experiments by Norman Farb at the University of Toronto seem to confirm that practising mindfulness can help bring us into a different way of relating with the world.[1] Farb and his colleagues demonstrated, using fMRI scans, that people appear to have two different modes of experience, each of which activates a different set of regions in the brain. One set drives the 'doing' mode. This is the part of us that focuses on narratives and concepts, rather than present-moment experience. It triggers areas of the brain such as the medial prefrontal cortex and the hippocampus, and seems to become active when we are telling ourselves stories about our lives, such as when we are running through plans about the future, or thinking about the past.

However, it seems there is another mode, which is based more on direct experience – a 'being', or experiential mode. When we operate in this way, several other parts of the brain seem to become active, such as the insula, which is implicated in the experience of bodily sensations, and the anterior cingulate cortex, which is known to be important in regulating attention. This mode – in which we focus primarily on the experience of the present moment – is the one in which we are more able to pay attention to how we are right now – it is the one in which we are mindful.

The 'doing' mode is not bad, of course – it is vital for us to be able to develop ideas and create stories that make sense of our experience, not to mention plan our next holiday or think about whom we are going to invite to our party – but without balancing this with the 'being' mode, we can find ourselves forever stuck in intellectualisation, always thinking about the past or the future, constantly theorising rather than also being able to switch into experiencing the 'now'.

What Farb and his colleagues have found, by doing fMRI scans on people's brains, is that those who have trained in mindfulness have a greater ability to shift consciously between these two networks, whereas people who had not received any training were more likely to default automatically into the 'doing' mode. As Mark Williams explains: 'It is as if the people who have been through mindfulness training have now learned a way to be with themselves in a more sensory, somatic way, without activating the stories about themselves.' Mindfulness, it seems, gives us greater choice about how we relate with the world – and as other neuroscientific studies of mindfulness suggest, we can train in developing more skilful ways of interacting with our experience. We can develop our capacity to be, as well as to do.

This will not happen overnight – mindfulness is a discipline we can practise throughout our lives, forever reminding ourselves to be present. We can always benefit from arousing our interest, sharpening our attention and cultivating kindness. Just as when we stop exercising we lose fitness, so stopping meditating can make it much easier for us to forget about being mindful and fall back into our more mind*less* habits again. But remember, it is not that your muscles have disappeared – they just need to be flexed a little to stay in shape!

A JOURNEY, NOT A RACE

It is interesting to notice what has changed, but remember, of course, not to get caught up in evaluation, which can easily become yet another self-judgement. If we go searching for the benefits of mindfulness practice, we are not yet being mindful, not yet resting in the present moment. It is something of a paradox – effort is required, but so is letting go of our ambition for any result.

This can be really hard for us in the West – we are so driven by doing, by succeeding and by achieving that we are always looking for a quick fix. You will notice a difference, for sure, but this is a process, a path, and if you fixate on a particular result you may miss out on something far more interesting that is just around the next corner. You are also likely to set yourself up for a lot of disappointment when you are unable to maintain your practice or you fall back into old patterns. The risk then is that you feel you have failed, and give up. This is not helpful – every single one of us, no matter how hard we practise or how wise we are, will get distracted at times. If just staying with our breath for longer than a couple of minutes while sitting in a quiet room is tough, then how much harder is it to bring mindfulness into our busy day-to-day lives?

The point is not to get hung up on perfection and lost in guilt when you forget; just come back to your breath and start again. This requires courage – if you are riding a horse you don't have to be brave to stay in the saddle, it's the getting back up when you've fallen off that takes guts. As you must by now be aware, mindfulness is not about getting rid of thoughts, of feelings, of pain – it is about changing your relationship with them – so just keep letting go and coming back to your breath, letting go and coming back, letting go and coming back …

When we practise, we are committing to a process of ongoing transformation, rather than a quick fix. This process of transformation is far, far more interesting than can be expressed by the scientific studies we have referred to. It is essential to question, to challenge and to try and understand our experience. Scientific research is one way of doing this, and it is important because it is scientific evidence that persuades decision-makers in our society that an approach is worth investing in. This mindfulness research is still in its early days – much more is needed if we are to understand precisely how it works, and how it can best reach the large number of people it might help. But the data provided by such research – which looks at events from an observational, outsider perspective – can never quite capture the rich, multi-layered experience that practising mindfulness can offer each individual practitioner. That is something that can only be discovered by making a different kind of investigation – a personal one, using your mind to look at your own experience.

Mindfulness can be much more than a technique to make us feel, think and act better – in the context of spiritual enquiry, mindfulness can be a quest to connect with reality in a way that cannot easily be measured by scientific trials. It is this context in which mindfulness has been practised for at least 2,500 years, certainly since the Buddha prescribed it as one aspect of his eightfold path, the basis for cultivating a way of being that leads towards enlightenment. It is one of the great benefits of mindfulness practice that it can be undertaken with different attitudes – for the scientifically-minded it can be a no-nonsense aid to wellbeing; for those of a more spiritual bent, it is a heartfelt, holistic approach to deep healing.

While more mindfulness may be useful in every situation, it is not a cure-all. In Buddhism there are a further seven aspects to the path (right view, right intention, right speech, right action, right livelihood, right effort and right concentration), and the fruits of positive psychology studies into wellbeing have found that there are many ingredients – not just mindfulness – that contribute to good mental health and a happier world. Some of these – connection, exercise, learning and being generous – were described in Chapter 4. Nevertheless, mindfulness is a strong foundation for wellbeing, a quality of awareness that helps us balance, integrate and work more skilfully with every aspect of life – our bodies, minds, emotions, and the external world. It can help us not just individually, but as families, communities, countries, and as a whole planet. If we can be mindful, we perhaps have a greater chance of manifesting happiness. That possibility is at the heart of the Mindful Manifesto.

THE MANIFESTO

Just 'be' for a moment – focus your attention on what is happening in your body, in your mind, in the world around you. Be inquisitive about whatever your experience is, and allow yourself to slow down enough to notice.

To help become fully aware of the remarkable experience of being alive, take some time every day to be mindful of your breath.

Practise being mindful of your body – reconnecting mind and body can allow us to experience a wholeness of being and help prevent and treat physical illness.

Notice and nurture your mind – by being mindful of your mind, you can train in living more happily, and help protect yourself from problems like depression and anxiety.

Work with your emotions mindfully, and begin to free yourself from the bonds of addiction. The more we are mindful of our feelings, the more we can open up to the miracle of the moment.

Open your eyes and extend your awareness – bring mindfulness into your life to become more skilful in every situation, and help to create a more mindful world.

WHERE TO NOW?

FURTHER READING AND RESOURCES

Hopefully, *The Mindful Manifesto* has given you a taste of what the practice of mindfulness involves, where it has come from, and how we could all benefit from incorporating it into our lives.

If you are interested in exploring mindfulness further, there are a number of other resources to explore, but it is important to remember that this isn't just a theoretical subject, but a way of being with practice at its heart. The exercises offered in this, and many other books, will give you a glimpse of this practice, but we would suggest you gain some personal experience by learning from an experienced guide. There are many MBSR and MBCT courses available across the UK – and you will find some of them listed on the Mental Health Foundation's mindfulness website (www.bemindful.co.uk). There is currently no agreed formal accreditation process that qualifies people to teach these courses, but if you want some guidance as to what is considered good practice to inform you in your choice of course, you can find it at http://www.bangor.ac.uk/mindfulness/.

If you suffer with depression, anxiety or any of a number of other mental health conditions, then mindfulness-based treatments may be available to you locally on the NHS via your GP. Although provision of these treatments remains somewhat patchy across the UK, this is changing all the time, so it is definitely worth talking to your GP or local PCT about how you might access approaches such as MBCT.

Another option is to look out for courses on meditation run by Buddhist centres – if you have one near you. These are often free and don't always mean you have to learn about Buddhism – although if this interests you then there is a lot to be said for embedding mindfulness practice in some sort of ongoing learning and study. There are a number of Buddhist traditions in which it is possible to engage in many aspects of the teaching and training of mindfulness and meditation, without having to call yourself a Buddhist.

THE MINDFUL MANIFESTO – ONLINE

Support the Mindful Manifesto by visiting our website at www.themindfulmanifesto.com. The site will connect you to the latest mindfulness news, as well as upcoming talks, courses and other offerings – and you can also order or download audio versions of the exercises from the book to help you in your practice. Plus, you can sign up for our regular blog and newsletter, as well as contact us. We'd love to hear from you about ways we could work together to create a more mindful world, or if you just want to tell us your experience of the manifesto and how you're applying it to your life.

OTHER SUGGESTED BOOKS

Sharon Begley, *The Plastic Mind* (Ballantine Books, 2007)

Pema Chodron, *When Things Fall Apart: Heart Advice for Difficult Times* (Shambhala Publications, 1997)

Daniel Goleman, *Destructive Emotions* (Bantam Books, 2003)

Thich Nhat Hanh, *The Miracle of Mindfulness: The Classic Guide to Meditation by the World's Most Revered Master* (Rider, 1991)

Dr Russ Harris, *The Happiness Trap: Stop Struggling, Start Living* (Exile Publishing, 2007)

Jon Kabat-Zinn, *Full Catastrophe Living: How to Cope with Stress, Pain and Illness Using Mindfulness Meditation* (Dell Publishing, 1991)

------, *Wherever You Go, There You are: Mindfulness Meditation for Everyday Life* (Hyperion Books, 1994)

Sakyong Mipham, *Turning the Mind into an Ally* (Riverhead Books, 2003)

Shanida Nataraja, *The Blissful Brain: Neuroscience and Proof of the Power of Meditation* (Gaia/Octopus Publishing, 2008)

Matthieu Ricard, *Happiness: A Guide to Developing Life's Most Important Skill* (NiL editions, 2003)

Spencer Smith and Steven C. Hayes, *Get Out of Your Mind and into Your Life: The New Acceptance and Commitment Therapy* (New Harbinger Publications, 2005)

Chögyam Trungpa, *Shambhala: The Sacred Path of the Warrior* (Shambhala Publications, 1984)

Mark Williams, John Teasdale, Zindel Segal, Jon Kabat-Zinn, *The Mindful Way through Depression: Freeing Yourself from Chronic Unhappiness* (includes Guided Meditation Practices CD; Guilford Press, 2007)

OTHER SUGGESTED WEBSITES

www.bemindful.co.uk
The Mental Health Foundation's website devoted to mindfulness, which includes a database of courses available throughout the UK. The Foundation has also developed a four-week online mindfulness course, details of which are on the same site

www.mbct.co.uk
Contains lots of useful information about mindfulness-based cognitive therapy

www.gaiahouse.co.uk
For those looking for a more intensive meditation experience, this Buddhist centre in Devon runs retreats throughout the year

www.bangor.ac.uk/mindfulness
Website of the University of Bangor Centre for Mindfulness Research and Practice

www.getsomeheadspace.com
This site is run by Andy Puddicombe, a meditation teacher who has developed a dynamic secular approach. It includes short exercises you can try, with great animations to go with them

THANKS

The contents of this book have been inspired by both ancient wisdom and modern research. It is, therefore, only thanks to the patience and generosity of many millions of people that we have access to such a huge and growing wealth of information on mindfulness and meditation. We would particularly like to thank those people who have generously given their knowledge and time during the preparation of this book – mindfulness experts such as Mark Williams, Sara Lazar, Alan Wallace, Paramabandhu Groves and Michael Chaskalson. Also invaluable have been our 'case studies', who've allowed us to share their experiences of mindfulness practice – we hope their stories are as inspiring to you as they are to us.

We have both been lucky enough to encounter the teachings of Chögyam Trungpa Rinpoche and the Sakyong Mipham Rinpoche, along with many other skilful, authentic teachers in the Shambhala Buddhist tradition, whose understanding and connection to teachings on mindfulness has offered us a path of enquiry along which we continue to stumble!

Thanks also to the fabulous team at Hay House, who responded so favourably to our idea for this book and who have helped steer it through to publication. We would especially like to thank our editor, Carolyn Thorne, who has been an unflappable and encouraging presence whenever we started to flap or get disheartened, our copy editor Barbara Vesey for skillfully refining our words, Joanna Lincoln for managing them into print, Jessica Crockett, Jo Burgess, Jo Lal, Nicola Fletcher, Monica Meehan and Samantha Hart for all their efforts to promote the book, publisher Michelle Pilley for her belief in it, and editorial assistant Amy Kiberd for her excellent support.

Ed: I'm profoundly grateful to all those who have helped me on my own ongoing meditation journey. There are far too many to name here, but in particular my meditation instructors Tom Dillon, Yves Bret and Caroline Helm have been patient, fearless, kind and endlessly encouraging. I'd also like to thank all those who have lived, worked and practised at the Dechen Choling retreat centre in France, where I spent a year deepening my meditation experience in 2006. Thanks also to my parents, Jill and Ivor Halliwell, who were instrumental in nurturing my early interest in existential questions, and to Rex Bradley, who has offered frequent wise guidance in recent years.

Thanks as well to everyone at the Mental Health Foundation, who responded so positively to the suggestion of a research project on mindfulness, disseminated its results so effectively, and kindly allowed me to reproduce some of the case studies used in this book. Gratitude also goes to Steph Ebdon, my agent, who has offered good advice of various kinds.

Above all, I'd like to thank my wonderful wife Victoria, who achieved the miraculously mindful feat of putting up with and encouraging me during the writing process. My share of this book is dedicated from my heart to hers.

Jonty: I'm indebted to all those who have encouraged and taught me over the last 38 years. Their generosity and kindness has allowed me not only to gain from their understanding and insight but also to grow in confidence in my own inherent wisdom, so that I have been able to believe that I have something interesting to say! In particular I want to thank those people who have, without criticism, pushed me to 'raise my gaze' and broaden my horizon, letting me glimpse what words like 'helping', 'caring' and 'healing' really mean – beyond the narrow confines of a purely biological model of health and illness. While at medical school I was fortunate enough to meet Eric Shepherd and Simon Read, who are really responsible for starting this process of exploration off. Then, as I embarked on my training to become a GP, I had the example of those such as David Poole, Roger Higgs, Annalee Curran and Tina Buchannan – all of whom continue to inspire me to be the best doctor that I can be.

I am indebted to Jim O'Neill and Peter Conradi, whose love and guidance have transformed the lives of a great many of the people they have taught, mine being just one of them. And to Julien Diaz for reminding me to take care of my body occasionally as well!

I also owe a huge debt of gratitude to my partners and all the staff at Manor Place Surgery. They know what it is to care, genuinely and deeply, for the patients they look after. I feel lucky to be a part of the team, and I thank them for the stability and support they offer me. It is this that has allowed me to branch out in so many different directions over recent years in the sure knowledge that if, and when, I lose sight of what is important they will be there to bring what really matters back into focus. And, of course, equally important in this process are the many patients who have worked, and continue to work, alongside me in taking care of their hearts, minds and bodies, and from whom I have learned so much. Helping is always a two-way street and the generosity of my patients in sharing their pain is a gift, not a burden, and one that gives me inspiration and sustenance without which my life would be all the poorer.

My share of this book would not have been possible without the love and support of my friends and family who have been so accepting of my constant preoccupation with writing it, and have come to know better than most that theory does not always translate into practice when it comes to being mindful! Although their contribution to the process does, of course, go much deeper than simply that of kindly onlookers. I am sure I am not unique in wanting to thank my parents, Frank and Rosemary, for all their love and support throughout my life – the sacrifices they have made so that I could have the opportunities I have had are truly humbling and a great inspiration to me.

And finally, love and thanks to my partner Tye who, despite being thousands of miles away for a lot of the time I have been writing this book, has spent many hours engaged in long trans-Atlantic phone calls calming and encouraging me and, without whom, my world would be a much less inspiring place.

REFERENCES

CHAPTER 1

1. Mental Health Foundation (2009). 'In the face of fear: how fear and anxiety affect our health and society, and what we can do about it', available at http://www.mentalhealth.org.uk/campaigns/mental-health-action-week-2009/in-the-face-of-fear/

2. 'Is Humanity Drowning in a Sea of Gadgets?', available at http://www.iforms.ltd.uk/news/it_technology/article_detail.php?article=6247&title=is-humanity-drowning-in-a-sea-of-gadgets

3. http://www.depression-primarycare.co.uk/where.htm

4. http://news.bbc.co.uk/1/hi/8230549.stm

5. V R Aggarwal *et al.* (2006). 'The epidemiology of chronic syndromes that are frequently unexplained: Do they have common associated factors?', *International Journal of Epidemiology* 35 (2): 468–76

6. For the full survey results, see Mental Health Foundation (2010). *Mindfulness Report* (London: Mental Health Foundation)

7. For an overview of mindfulness and its use for mental health problems, see Mental Health Foundation (2010). *Mindfulness Report* (London: Mental Health Foundation)

CHAPTER 2

1. For an overview of the Four Noble Truths, see http://www.bbc.co.uk/religion/religions/buddhism/beliefs/fournobletruths_1.shtml

2. See 'Liposuction will give me confidence', available at http://news.bbc.co.uk/1/hi/health/8189227.stm and 'Recession cuts many, not all plastic surgery procedures', available at http://www.sciencedaily.com/releases/2009/03/090325132534.htm

3. Sakyong Mipham Rinpoche (2004). *Turning the Mind into an Ally* (New York: Riverhead)

4. For a full translated text of the Four Foundations of Mindfulness, see, for example, http://www.accesstoinsight.org/lib/authors/nyansatta/wheel019.html or http://www.buddhanet.net/imol/foudatn.htm

5. William James (1890). *The Principles of Psychology* (New York: Holt): 401

6. Sigmund Freud, quoted in J Austin (1999). *Zen and the Brain: Toward an Understanding of Meditation and Consciousness* (Cambridge, MA: MIT Press): 127

7. For more on Albert Ellis, visit the Albert Ellis Institute at http://www.rebt.org/

8. This is from the opening lines of the Dhammapada: 'We are what we think/All that we are arises with

our thoughts/With our thoughts we make the world/ Speak or act with an impure mind/And trouble will follow you/As the wheel follows the ox that draws the cart/We are what we think/All that we are arises with our thoughts/With our thoughts we make the world' quoted at http://www.thebigview.com/buddhism/dhammapada-01.html

9. E Sternberg (2009). *Healing Spaces: The Science of Place and Well-being* (Cambridge, MA: Harvard University Press): 111–14

10. Maguire *et al.* (2000). 'Navigation-related structural change in the hippocampi of taxi drivers', *Proceedings of the National Academy of Sciences* 97(8): 4398–4403

11. See, for example, 'Learning Languages "Boosts Brain"' available at http://news.bbc.co.uk/1/hi/health/3739690.stm

12. B Johannson (2006). 'Music and brain plasticity', *European Review* 14(1): 49–64

13. S Begley (2007). *Train Your Mind, Change Your Brain: How a new science reveals our extraordinary potential to transform ourselves* (New York: Ballantine Books)

14. See, for example, Kahneman *et al.* (2004). 'Toward National Well-being Accounts', available at http://www.krueger.princeton.edu/Toward%20Well-being.pdf

15. For more on the work of Professor Davidson, see the laboratory's website at http://psyphz.psych.wisc.edu/

16. For more, see D Goleman (2003). 'Finding Happiness: Cajole Your Brain to Lean to the Left', *New York Times*, available at http://www.nytimes.com/2003/02/04/health/behavior-finding-happiness-cajole-your-brain-to-lean-to-the-left.html?pagewanted=1; also, R J Davidson and W Irwin (1999). 'The functional neuroanatomy of emotion and affective style', *Trends in Cognitive Sciences* 3(1): 11–21

17. R J Davidson *et al.* (2003). 'Alterations in Brain and Immune Function Produced by Mindfulness Meditation', *Psychosomatic Medicine* 65: 564–70

18. S Lazar *et al.* (2005). 'Meditation experience is associated with increased cortical thickness', *Neuroreport* 16(17): 1893–97

19. E Luders *et al.* (2009). 'The underlying anatomical correlates of long-term meditation: Larger hippocampal and frontal volumes of gray matter', *NeuroImage* 45(3): 672–78

CHAPTER 3

1. See http://www.rethink.org/living_with_mental_illness/everyday_living/physical_health_and_wellbeing/staying_healthy/index.html

2. See, for example, 'MIND on Pain: When Pain Lingers,' *Scientific American Mind*, Sep 2009, at http://www.scientificamerican.com/article.cfm?id=when-pain-lingers

3. A J Barsky and J F Borus (1995). 'Somatization and Medicalization in the Era of Managed Care', *Journal of the American Medical Association* 274(24): 1931–34

4. For more in-depth discussion of how meditation and other Buddhist practices can affect brain and body systems, see R Hanson (2009). *Buddha's Brain: The Practical Neuroscience of Happiness, Love and Wisdom* (New Harbinger). There are also some excellent resources on the author's website, http://www.rickhanson.net

5. See, for example, BBC News (2004). 'Stress "may speed up cell ageing"', at http://news.bbc.co.uk/1/hi/4054207.stm

6. R K Wallace *et al.* (1982). 'The effects of the transcendental meditation and tm-sidhi program on the aging process', *International Journal of Neuroscience* 16(1): 53–58

7. Quoted in J Austin (2009). *Selfless Insight: Zen and the Meditative Transformations of Consciousness* (Cambridge, MA: MIT Press): 8

8. D Cioffi and J Holloway (1993). 'Delayed costs of suppressed pain', *Journal of Personality and Social Psychology* 64: 274–82

9. For some comprehensive reviews, see Grossman *et al.* (2004). 'Mindfulness-based stress reduction and health benefits: A meta-analysis', *Journal of Psychosomatic*

Research 57(1): 35–43; Brown *et al.* (2007).
'Mindfulness: Theoretical foundations and evidence for
its salutary effects', *Psychological Inquiry* 18(4): 211–37;
Baer *et al.* (2003) 'Mindfulness Training as a Clinical
Intervention: A Conceptual and Empirical Review',
Clinical Psychology: Science and Practice 10(2): 138

10. B Roth and T Creaser (1997). 'Mindfulness meditation-
based stress reduction: experience with a bilingual
inner-city program', *Nurse Practitioner* 5: 215

11. J Kabat-Zinn *et al.* (1992). 'Effectiveness of a
meditation-based stress reduction program in the
treatment of anxiety disorders', *American Journal of
Psychiatry* 149: 936–43

12. J Kabat-Zinn *et al.* (1985). 'The clinical use of
mindfulness meditation for the self-regulation of
chronic pain', *Journal of Behavioral Medicine* 8(2)

13. J Kabat-Zinn *et al.* (1998). 'Influence of a mindfulness
meditation-based stress reduction intervention on
rates of skin clearing in patients with moderate to
severe psoriasis undergoing phototherapy (UVB) and
photochemotherapy (PUVA)', *Psychosomatic Medicine*
60(5): 625–32

14. L Witek-Janusek (2008). 'Effect of mindfulness-based
stress reduction on immune function, quality of life
and coping in women newly diagnosed with early stage
breast cancer', *Brain, Behavior and Immunity* 22(6):
968–81

15. J D Creswell *et al.* (2009). 'Mindfulness meditation training effects on CD4+ T lymphocytes in HIV-1 infected adults: A small randomized controlled trial', *Brain, Behavior and Immunity* 23(2): 184–88

16. J Kabat-Zinn (1982). 'An outpatient program in behavioural medicine for chronic pain patients based on the practice of Mindfulness meditation: theoretical considerations and preliminary results', *General Hospital Psychiatry* 4(1): 334; L M McCracken, J Gauntlett-Gilbert and K E Vowles (2007). 'The role of Mindfulness in a contextual cognitive behavioral analysis of chronic pain-related suffering and disability', *Pain* 131: 63–69

17. Based on extrapolating from US figures, which suggest medically unexplained illnesses account for 16 per cent of all healthcare costs, see J A Barsky *et al.* (2005). 'Somatisation Increases Medical Utilisation and Costs Independent of Psychiatric and Medical Comorbidity', *Archives of General Psychiatry* 62: 903–10

18. See, for example, R Morris and L Gask (2008). 'Assessment and immediate management of patients with medically unexplained symptoms in primary care and general hospital settings', *The Foundation Years* 4(2): 59–63

19. See R A Baer (2003). 'Mindfulness training as a clinical intervention: a conceptual and empirical review', *Clinical Psychology Science & Practice* 10: 125–43

CHAPTER 4

1. For more statistics on the prevalence of mental health problems, see Mental Health Foundation (2007). *The Fundamental Facts: The Latest Facts and Figures on Mental Health* (London: Mental Health Foundation)

2. See BBC News (2009). 'Depression looms as global crisis', at http://news.bbc.co.uk/1/hi/health/8230549.stm

3. See Mental Health Foundation (2007) *The Fundamental Facts: The Latest Facts and Figures on Mental Health* (London: Mental Health Foundation)

4. Ibid.

5. For example, see 'Does Depression Shrink Your Brain?', available at http://abcnews.go.com/Health/Depression/story?id=3885728&page=2

6. Ibid.

7. See New Economics Foundation (2004). *A Well-being Manifesto for a Flourishing Society*, available at www.wellbeingmanifesto.net/uk_manifesto.pdf

8. See *Five Ways to Well-being*, available at http://www.neweconomics.org/projects/five-ways-well-being

9. See http://www.neweconomics.org/projects/five-ways-well-being

10. Z Segal, J Teasdale and M Williams (2002). *Mindfulness-based cognitive therapy for depression: a new approach to preventing relapse* (New York: The Guilford Press): 28

11. J D Teasdale, Z V Segal, J M G Williams *et al.* (2000). 'Prevention of relapse/recurrence in major depression by Mindfulness-based cognitive therapy', *Journal of Consulting and Clinical Psychology* 68: 615–23

12. S H Ma and J D Teasdale (2004). 'Mindfulness-based cognitive therapy for depression: replication and exploration of differential relapse prevention effects', *Journal of Consulting and Clinical Psychology* 72: 31–40

13. W Kuyken, S Byford, R S Taylor *et al.* (2008). 'Mindfulness-based cognitive therapy to prevent relapse in recurrent depression', *Journal of Consulting and Clinical Psychology* 76(6): 966–78

14. See T Barnhofer, C Crane, E Hargus *et al.* (2009). 'Mindfulness-based cognitive therapy as a treatment for chronic depression: a preliminary study', *Behaviour Research and Therapy* 47(5): 366–73; M Kenny and J M G Williams (2007). 'Treatment-resistant depressed patients show a good response to Mindfulness-based cognitive therapy', *Behaviour Research and Therapy* 45(3): 617–25; S J Eisendrath, K Delucchi, R Bitner *et al.* (2008). 'Mindfulness-based cognitive therapy for treatment-resistant depression: a pilot study', *Psychotherapy & Psychosomatics* 77: 319–20

15. For an overview of mindfulness and its use for mental health problems, see Mental Health Foundation (2010). *Mindfulness Report* (London: Mental Health Foundation)

16. Ibid.

17. See Chögyam Trungpa, *The Education of the Warrior*, available at http://www.poetry-chaikhana.com/T/ TrungpaChogy/EducationofW.htm

18. For evidence on the qualities shown by more mindful people, see, for example, K Brown, R Ryan and D Cresswell (2007). 'Mindfulness: theoretical foundations and evidence for its salutary effects', *Psychological Inquiry* 18(4): 211–37; D Siegel (2007). *The Mindful Brain: Reflection and Attunement in the Cultivation of Wellbeing* (New York: W W Norton); J Williams (2008). 'Mindfulness, depression and modes of mind', *Cognitive Therapy and Research* 32(6): 721–33; P A Frewen, E M Evans, N Maraj *et al.* (2008). 'Letting go: Mindfulness and negative automatic thinking', *Cognitive Therapy and Research* 32(6): 758–74; W L Heppner and M H Kernis (2007). 'Quiet ego functioning: the complementary roles of Mindfulness, authenticity, and secure high self-esteem', *Psychological Inquiry* 18(4): 248–51; P R Shaver, S Lavy, C D Saron *et al.* (2007). 'Social foundations of the capacity for Mindfulness: an attachment perspective', *Psychological Inquiry* 18(4): 264–71

CHAPTER 5

1. J Bradshaw (1996). 'Bradshaw on the Family: A New Way of Creating Solid Self-Esteem', *Health Communications*: 108

2. See, for example, http://www.drugscope.org.uk/resources/drugsearch/drugsearchpages/tobacco

3. See http://news.bbc.co.uk/1/hi/magazine/4188071.stm

4. P Chodron (2005). *When Things Fall Apart: Heart Advice for Difficult Times* (London: Element): 15

5. See, for example, 'Anxiety and Stress Found to Promote Cocaine Use in Rats', National Institute On Drug Abuse, available at http://www.nida.nih.gov/NIDA_notes/NNVol11N4/Anxiety.html and 'Stress Changes Your Brain', at http://www.abc.net.au/rn/science/ss/stories/s802817.ht

6. See, for example, ScienCentral News, 'Stress Changes Your Brain', at http://www.salesbrain.net/articles/ScienCentral%20Stress%20Changes%20Your%20Brain.htm

7. See, for example, UCLA Center for Buddhist Studies, 'Psychology Study Finds Resonance with Buddhist Teachings', at http://www.international.ucla.edu/buddhist/article.asp?parentid=72539

8. C Trungpa (1996). *The Sacred Path of the Warrior* (Boston, MA: Shambhala Publications)

9. See K Brown, R Ryan and D Cresswell (2007). 'Mindfulness: theoretical foundations and evidence for its salutary effects', *Psychological Inquiry* 18(4): 211–37, and S S Welch, S Rizvi and S Dimijian (2006). 'Mindfulness in dialectical behaviour therapy (DBT) for borderline personality disorder', in R A Baer (ed) (2005). *Mindfulness-based treatment approaches: clinician's guide to evidence base and applications* (San Diego: Academic Press): 117–38

10. G A Marlatt *et al.* (1984). 'Effects of meditation and relaxation training upon alcohol misuse in male social drinkers', in D H Shapiro and R N Walsh (eds) (1984). *Meditation: Classic and Contemporary Perspectives* (New York: Aldine), and Murphy *et al.* (1986). 'Lifestyle Modification with Heavy Alcohol Drinkers: Effects of Aerobic Exercise and Meditation', *Addictive Behaviors* 11(2): 175–86

11. See, for example, 'Researchers see promise in treating addictive behaviors with mindfulness meditation', *Milwaukee-Wisconsin Journal Sentinel*, April 19 2010, at http://www.jsonline.com/features/health/91516249.html

12. S Bowen *et al.* (2006). 'Mindfulness Meditation and Substance Use in an Incarcerated Population', *Psychology of Addictive Behaviors* 20(3): 343–47

13. J M Davis (2007). 'A pilot study on mindfulness-based stress reduction for smokers', *BMC Complementary and Alternative Medicine* 7: 2

14. J L Kristeller, R A Baer and R Quillian-Wolever (2006). 'Mindfulness-based approaches to eating disorders', in R A Baer (ed) (2005). *Mindfulness-based Treatment Approaches: Clinician's Guide to Evidence Base and Applications* (San Diego: Academic Press): 75–93

CHAPTER 6

1. Kabat-Zinn's most often quoted full definition is: 'Paying attention in a particular way: on purpose, in the present moment, and nonjudgmentally'.

2. A Wallace (2006). *The Attention Revolution: Unlocking the Power of the Focused Mind* (Somerville, MA: Wisdom)

3. W Gallagher (2009). *Rapt: Attention and the Focused Life* (Harmondsworth: Penguin)

4. A P Jha, J Krompinger and M J Baime (2007). 'Mindfulness training modifies subsystems of attention', *Cognitive, Affective & Behavioral Neuroscience* 7: 109–19

5. H A Slagter, A Lutz, L L Greischar, A D Francis, S Nieuwenhuis *et al.* (2007). 'Mental Training Affects Distribution of Limited Brain Resources' *PLoS Biology* 5(6): e138. doi:10.1371/journal.pbio.0050138

6. Lisa T Cullen (2006). 'How to Get Smarter, One Breath at a Time: Scientists find that meditation not only reduces stress but also reshapes the brain', *Time* 16th January 2006, available at http://www.time.com/time/magazine/article/0,9171,1147167,00.html

7. E Luders (2009). 'The underlying anatomical correlates of long-term meditation: Larger hippocampal and frontal volumes of gray matter' *NeuroImage* 45(3): 672–78

8. For more on work-related stress, see http://www.cipd. co.uk/subjects/health/stress/stress.htm and http://www. healthyworkinglives.com/advice/work-relatedillness- injury/stress-workplace.aspx; Health and Safety Executive (2004). 'Helping business cut the cost of work-related stress', available at http://www.hse.gov.uk/ press/2004/c04046.htm

9. For a full description of Transport for London's use of mindfulness for their employees, see the case study in Mental Health Foundation (2010). *Mindfulness Report* (London: Mental Health Foundation): 70

10. J Dahl *et al.* (2004). 'Acceptance and commitment therapy and the treatment of persons at risk for long- term disability resulting from stress and pain symptoms: A preliminary randomized trial', *Behavior Therapy* 35(4): 785–801

11. See http://www.cipd.co.uk/subjects/health/stress/stress. htm

12. INSEAD (2007). 'Understanding and responding to societal demands on corporate responsibility (response). Final report', available at http://www.insead. edu/v1/ibis/response_project/documents/Response_ FinalReport.pdf

13. P E Flaxman and F W Bond (2006). 'Acceptance and commitment therapy in the workplace', in R A Baer (ed) (2005). *Mindfulness-based treatment approaches: clinician's guide to evidence base and applications* (San Diego: Academic Press): 377–82

14. M S Krasner *et al.* (2009). 'Association of an Educational Program in Mindful Communication with Burnout, Empathy, and Attitudes Among Primary Care Physicians', *Journal of the American Medical Association* 302(12): 1284–93

15. S L Shapiro, G E Schwartz, G Bonner (1998). 'Effects of Mindfulness-based stress reduction on medical and premedical students', *Journal of Behavioral Medicine* 21: 581–99

16. R J Semple, J Lee, L F Miller (2006). 'Mindfulness-based cognitive therapy for children', in R A Baer (ed) (2005). *Mindfulness-based Treatment Approaches: Clinician's Guide to Evidence Base and Applications* (San Diego: Academic Press): 143–65

17. See O Bowcott (2009). 'Tories slam doctors for drugging children', *The Guardian*, available at http://www.guardian.co.uk/society/2009/oct/30/conservatives-nhs-children-drugs-mental-health

18. C A Burke (2009). 'Mindfulness-Based Approaches with Children and Adolescents: A Preliminary Review of Current Research in an Emergent Field', *Journal of Child and Family Studies*, available at http://www.springerlink.com/content/e1638088141n327m/

19. C Vieten and J Astin (2008). 'Effects of a Mindfulness-based intervention during pregnancy on prenatal stress and mood: results of a pilot study', *Archives of Women's Mental Health* 1(1): 67–74

20. See K Brown, R Ryan and D Cresswell (2007). 'Mindfulness: theoretical foundations and evidence for its salutary effects', *Psychological Inquiry* 18(4): 211–37; D Siegel (2007). *The Mindful Brain: Reflection and Attunement in the Cultivation of Well-being* (New York: W W Norton); J Williams (2008). 'Mindfulness, depression and modes of mind', *Cognitive Therapy and Research* 32(6): 721–33; P A Frewen, E M Evans, N Maraj *et al.* (2008). 'Letting go: Mindfulness and negative automatic thinking', *Cognitive Therapy and Research* 32(6): 758–74; W L Heppner and M H Kernis (2007). 'Quiet ego functioning: the complementary roles of mindfulness, authenticity, and secure high self-esteem', *Psychological Inquiry* 18(4): 248–51; P R Shaver, S Lavy, C D Saron *et al.* (2007). 'Social foundations of the capacity for mindfulness: an attachment perspective', *Psychological Inquiry* 18(4): 264–71

21. D Siegel (2007). *The Mindful Brain: Reflection and Attunement in the Cultivation of Well-being* (New York: W W Norton)

22. J W Carson, K M Carson, K M Gil *et al.* (2006). 'Mindfulness-based relationship enhancement (MBRE) in couples', in R A Baer (ed) (2005). *Mindfulness-based Treatment Approaches: Clinician's Guide to Evidence Base and Applications* (San Diego: Academic Press): 309–29

23. C Blake (2010). *The Joy of Mindful Sex: Be in the Moment and Enrich Your Lovemaking* (Lewes: Ivy Press); L A Brotto *et al.* (2008). 'Eastern approaches for enhancing women's sexuality: Mindfulness, acupuncture, and yoga', *Journal of Sexual Medicine* 5: 2741–48; see also D Goldmeier and A J Mears (2010). 'Meditation: A Review of its Use in Western Medicine and, in Particular, its Role in the Management of Sexual Dysfunction', *Current Psychiatry Reviews* 6(1): 11–14

CONCLUSION

1. N Farb *et al.* (2007). 'Attending to the present: mindfulness meditation reveals distinct neural modes of self-reference', *Social Cognitive and Affective Neuroscience* 2(4): 313-22. For a good summary and explanation of this paper's findings, see D Rock (2009), 'The neuroscience of mindfulness', available at http://www.psychologytoday.com/blog/your-brain-work/200910/the-neuroscience-mindfulness

INDEX

Page numbers in **bold** refer to whole chapters.

THE MINDFUL MANIFESTO
– ONLINE

WWW.THEMINDFULMANIFESTO.COM

Support the Mindful Manifesto by visiting our website, where you'll find:

- all the latest mindfulness news, including details of our talks, courses, coaching and workshops

- audio versions of exercises from *The Mindful Manifesto*, to help you get started in your practice

- discussion of the latest developments in mindfulness, via the Mindful Manifesto blog

- details of how to sign up for our newsletter and contact us about our work.

MIND FUL NESS...

You've read the book and begun your mindfulness journey!

To help you explore and learn more about mindfulness, the Mental Health Foundation has launched an online mini-mindfulness course. The four week course teaches the core principles of mindfulness and uses videos, audio and online journals to enable you to practice mindfulness techniques at a pace, and in a place, that suits you.

Taught by qualified mindfulness practitioners, and supported by Bangor University, the course is a great way to take your next mindful step.

Visit **bemindful.co.uk** for more information.

Mental Health Foundation